2/5/63   (6a - 18415)

BRITAIN AND
SOUTH-EAST ASIA

By the same Author

*

SOCIALISM IN SOUTHERN ASIA

Published by the Oxford University Press
for The Royal Institute of International
Affairs, 1960

Also in the series

BRITAIN AND CHINA

by Evan Luard

BRITAIN AND
SOUTH-EAST ASIA

Saul Rose

THE JOHNS HOPKINS PRESS: BALTIMORE

Published in Great Britain by
Chatto & Windus Ltd
42 William IV Street
London W.C.2

Library of Congress Catalog Card Number: 62-18415

Acknowledgement

For their help in bringing this book to completion my grateful thanks are due to the Leverhulme Trust and its Director, Sir Miles Clifford, K.B.E.; to the Warden and Fellows of St. Antony's College; to all those authorities from whose knowledge I have profited, particularly Mr. Francis Carnell and the authors listed in the select bibliography; to Mrs. Anne Liley; and to my wife. For the defects that remain I alone am responsible.

St. Antony's College,   S. R.
Oxford   February, 1962

Contents

Introduction   *page* 9

EXPANSION

1 Reconnaissance and Retreat   15
2 Return   27

BETWEEN THE WARS

3 Cash Nexus   61
4 Cultural Links   67
5 Political Framework   76
6 Strategy at Singapore   83

WAR AND WITHDRAWAL

7 Japan's New Order   95
8 Burma   109
9 Malaya   126
10 Singapore   139
11 Borneo   147
12 Further South and East   157

PRESENT AND FUTURE

13 Aid and Trade   171
14 Strategy and Politics   181
15 Retrospect and Prospect   195
   Select Bibliography   200
   Index   203

Maps

English Voyages up to 1600	*facing page* 16
British Factories 1600–1623	20
British Factories 1623–1785	27
British Acquisitions 1786–1824	39
British Possessions 1826	41
British Expansion 1826–52	44
British Dependencies 1852–1888	55
British Dependencies 1914	59
Malaya 1914	79
Boundaries of SEAC before and after the Japanese surrender	109

INTRODUCTION

"CROSSROADS" is a word which comes readily to mind when considering south-east Asia. It is very much an in-between region, whether viewed from land or sea. It lies between the Indian Ocean and the Pacific, between Asia and Australasia, between the Indian subcontinent and China. Indo-China, the name of part of the region, could be applied to the whole. The term "south-east Asia" carries a similar connotation—of the hyphen between south and east.

During its long history the crossroads has seen a great deal of traffic. Although the discovery of Java Man—the remains of the earliest known form of human being—suggests that it was one of the birthplaces of mankind, the region has been moulded largely by external forces. For thousands of years successive waves of migrants moved down from the Asian continent towards the south, driven by the hostility of nature or their neighbours, or perhaps drawn by the warmth and luxuriance of the tropics. They made their way from the interior of the "heartland" down towards the Malay peninsula, some settling, some moving on along the island chain that constitutes Indonesia, until they reached the Philippines or even Australia. The last major influx occurred some 4,000 years ago with the arrival of the people who still constitute what may be described as the basic population of the area—the Malaysians—but they were not very numerous. Although the mountain ranges run broadly north and south, the broken terrain and the dense malarial jungles impeded movement, and the migrations were a trickle rather than a flood. In comparison with India and China the region remained thinly populated until the fairly recent proliferation in Java.

At the beginning of the Christian era trade with India and China was well established. References are to be found in ancient Indian writings—the Ramayana and the Puranas—while the Chinese annals record the reception of embassies bearing tribute. Except in Tongking, which bordered on China, the Indian impact was much the stronger. The Indians brought with them Hinduism and Buddhism, Sanskrit and other aspects of their culture. The great temples of Borobodur in Java and Angkor in Cambodia are awe-inspiring monuments to its quality. Traders settled and became the nucleus of Indian influence. The kingdom of Funan in Cambodia was said to have been founded in the first century A.D. by a Brahmin. The adjacent kingdom of Champa which rose in the next century was also "Indianized", as was Langkasuka in the north of the Malay peninsula.

In these early times, when the skills of navigation and shipbuilding were less developed, traders tended to take a short cut overland by the Kra isthmus rather than sail round the Malay peninsula; and this may account for the location of the earlier Indianized states. Later, as techniques improved the longer sea route became less intimidating, and other Indianized empires arose among the islands to the south—first, Srivijaya, based on Sumatra, which lasted from the eighth to the fourteenth century, when it was overthrown and supplanted by the empire of Majapahit, based on Java, soon to be eclipsed in its turn by the rise of Malacca. Meanwhile, the movement down from the north continued. The Burmese descended the Irrawaddy valley to the lowlands, overcame the Mons who were already there, and established their kingdom at Pagan. The Thai followed them on a more easterly track, and set up their capital at Ayuthia, exerting such pressure on the neighbouring Khmers as to compel them eventually to abandon the splendour of Angkor to the encroaching jungle. Further east still, the Annamites filtered down the Indo-Chinese peninsula. All these groups contributed to the ethnic kaleidoscope which was to make south-east Asia the habitat of "plural societies".

In addition to these overspills there were two major incursions into the region by Imperial China. In the thirteenth century the armies of the Mongol dynasty overran Annam and invaded Burma. That indefatigable traveller Marco Polo was an eye-witness to the victory of the Mongols over the Burmese. A Mongol expedition penetrated southward as far as Java but was obliged to withdraw. The Ming dynasty which succeeded the Mongols in the fourteenth century was also expansionist at first. Annam was conquered, and Chinese fleets exacted tribute from Java, Sumatra and Malacca. Then the policy of seclusion was adopted and once again the region was subjected to influences coming from the West.

Just as, earlier, Indian traders had brought with them Hinduism and Buddhism, so in the fourteenth century Gujerati or Bengali traders brought Islam. The new creed took root and flourished where it was adopted by local rulers, the most important convert in the fifteenth century being the ruler of Malacca. The rapid growth in the wealth, power and influence of that port helped to carry the faith far and wide on the Malay peninsula and in the archipelago.

Throughout the fifteenth century trade from the East to the Red Sea and the Persian Gulf was in Muslim hands. The goods were transported overland to the Mediterranean coast for distribution to their European destinations. This meant that all consignments changed hands several times in transit. The European voyages of discovery aimed partly at finding a way to circumvent this cumbersome and costly method of commerce, at a time when the flow of trade through the Middle East was threatened by the rise of the Ottoman Turks.

The Portuguese were the first to succeed in turning the flank of Africa. The arrival of Vasco da Gama at Calicut in India in 1498, in search of Christians and spices, heralded the era of European dominance in Asia. The first steps for the Portuguese were to secure command of the seas and establish bases. The capture of Goa in 1510 provided an effective centre from which to control the Indian trade, and the conquest of Malacca in the following year extended their sway to south-east Asia. For the remainder of the century the Portuguese were able to sustain and develop their monopoly of trade, and the conquest of Malacca in the following year extended where Spain succeeded in gaining a foothold. The effort placed a great strain on the resources of that tiny country and their supremacy could not be maintained. When the kingdoms of Spain and Portugal were united under one crown, the Netherlands rose in revolt; and in their struggle for independence the Dutch sought to break the grip of the Portuguese on the East Indian trade.

It was in this setting that the English made their appearance in south-east Asia.

EXPANSION

I

RECONNAISSANCE AND RETREAT

AS the sixteenth century and the reign of Queen Elizabeth I drew to their close, the exuberant energy of the Elizabethan era spilled over into yet another area of the globe. In their search for trade some London merchants turned their eyes towards south-east Asia. In the year 1599 a group of them petitioned the Queen for her assent to a voyage to the East Indies, prompted as they said by the success of their Dutch competitors:

". . . divers merchants, induced by the successe of the viage performed by the Duche Nation, and being informed that the Duchemen prepare for a new viage, and to that ende have bought divers ships here, in Englande, were stirred with no lesse affection to advaunce the trade of their native countrie than ye Duche merchaunts were to benefite theire commonwealthe, and upon that affeccion have resolved to make a viage to the East Indies."

In response to this petition a royal charter was granted, and the East India Company came into being on December 31, 1600.

The quest for Eastern trade had been proceeding throughout most of the sixteenth century, and attempts had been made to find the north-west or north-east passage to China. Drake's voyage round the world (1577–80) was not merely for the purpose of plundering Spanish treasure ships: its ostensible object was discovery and trade in the Pacific. Drake touched at Ternate in the Moluccas and brought back a cargo of cloves and a treaty with the king of the island. In England even more importance was attached to the treaty than to the treasure.

At first, the English interest in trade with the Indies was marginal. What the English merchants were looking for was not so much a supply of the produce of the East as a market for English manufactures, especially woollen goods, which were not likely to find a ready sale in the tropics. Hence the search for markets in colder climes, particularly China. This preference, however, should not be pressed too far: for there were some products of the Indies which were in constant demand in England, notably pepper and

15

spices to season the meat which had to be preserved for the winter. But the main object was to sell, not to buy, as declared by Hakluyt:

"Because our chiefe desire is to find out ample vent of our wollen cloth (the naturall commoditie of this our realme) the fittest places . . . are the manifold islands of Japan and the northern parts of China and the regions of the Tartars next adjoining."

The trade that could be obtained in the Indies was at first regarded as incidental to this major objective.

A perceptible change of attitude followed the capture by Drake in 1587 of a Portuguese carrack, the *San Filippe*, with a cargo from the East Indies worth more than £100,000. Hakluyt Hakluyt:

". . . the taking of this carak wrought two extraordinary effects in England: first, that it taught others that caracks were no such bugs but they might be taken . . . and secondly, in acquainting the English Nation more generally with the particularities of the exceeding riches and wealth of the East Indies; whereby themselves and their neighbours of Holland have been incouraged (being men as skilfull in navigation and of no lesse courage then the Portugals) to share with them in the East Indies, where their strength is nothing so great as heretofore hath been supposed."

Further information about the riches of the Indies was provided by Ralph Fitch after his journey via the Middle East and overland across India (1583–91). He penetrated as far as Pegu in Burma, Chiengmai in Siam, and Malacca on the Malay peninsula, and brought back a report of the exotic commodities that could be obtained, among them pepper, ginger, cloves, nutmegs, mace, white sandalwood, camphor, aloes, benjamin, long pepper, musk, amber, rubies, sapphires, diamonds and pearls. It was clear, however, that these goods could not be carried by the route he had travelled.

The alternative was the sea route round the Cape of Good Hope which was used by the Portuguese. Hitherto the English had not attempted it for several reasons. One was lack of knowledge, both of geography and navigation, which the Portuguese tried to keep as their own preserve. There was also little interest, as the East Indies

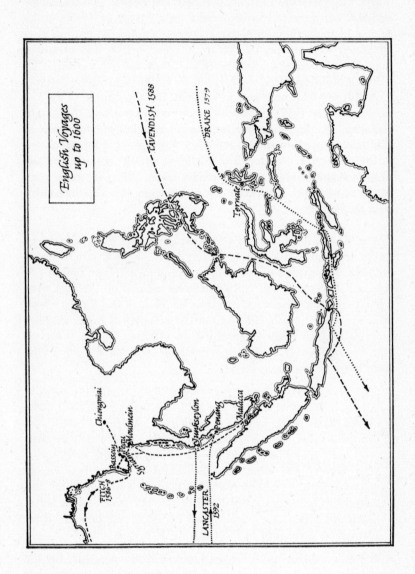

English Voyages
up to 1600

CAVENDISH 1588

DRAKE 1579

Ternate

Chiengmai

Bassein

Pegu
Syriam
Martaban

Junkceylon

Penang

Malacca

FITCH
1586-8

LANCASTER
1592

B

did not seem to offer a promising market for English manufactures. There was a dearth of capital, for a considerable amount of money and risk was involved in embarking on a voyage of 16,000 miles to deal in spices. Shipping, too, presented a difficulty. English merchantmen were usually of 200 to 300 tons, which was an uneconomic size for so long a voyage. The Portuguese had met this difficulty by building carracks of 1,200 to 1,500 tons. These carracks looked formidable and were a deterrent. But the capture of the *San Filippe* showed that the carracks "were no such bugs but they might be taken" by the much smaller English vessels, and the union of Portugal with Spain since 1580 made Portuguese shipping a legitimate target for plunder. The challenge of the Spanish Armada prompted the English to build bigger ships, and more knowledge of the route to the East became available from men who had sailed with the Portuguese.

The East India Company's first voyage, under the command of James Lancaster, sailed in 1601 for Achin at the northern tip of Sumatra. It consisted of four ships ranging in size from 600 to 240 tons and in complement from 200 to 80 men. With the fleet went a letter from the Queen addressed to the rulers of the ports at which the ships might touch, holding out the prospect of better supplies through English agents than had been afforded by the Spaniards and Portuguese. If the ruler wished to continue the trade, the royal letter affirmed:

> "We have given order to this our principal merchant to leave in your country some such of our said merchants as he shall make choice of, to reside in your dominions, under your princely and safe protection, until the return of another fleet which we shall send unto you, who may in the meantime learn the language of your country and apply their behaviour as it may best sort to converse with your Majesty's subjects to the end that, amity and friendship being entertained and begun, the same may be better continued when our people shall be instructed how to direct themselves according to the fashions of your country."

It was no doubt useful as the Queen's letter indicated, for the traders to learn the language and the customs of the country; but there was a further practical consideration. If trade were confined to the brief duration of the fleet's visit there would be a strong incentive for the local inhabitants to agree to make low bids for the ships' cargo while demanding high prices for their own produce. But if there was a "factor" on the spot all the year round he could pick the best time to sell and buy, and collect the produce of the country in his "factory" for the next Company ship that called.

The first of these English factories was established at Bantam in Java by Lancaster. His four ships returned with full cargoes of spices, so the voyage was a success—but not as profitable as it might have been, for they brought back so much pepper as to cause a glut on the market.

The hazards of navigation and the Portuguese now appeared to have been successfully overcome; but a new difficulty appeared in the shape of competition from the Dutch who aimed at establishing a monopoly of the spice trade and were prepared to employ much greater resources to do so. In consequence, the subsequent voyages of the Company were often squeezed out of potential trading ports by strong Dutch fleets which obtained exclusive treaties from the local rulers. This was all the more annoying because the Company soon discovered an effective way of trading with the East Indies by means of the produce of India. Its factors in the Indies reported that there was a great demand for Indian cloth and calico which could be exchanged very profitably for pepper and finer spices. Indian opium, too, found a ready market. This discovery, together with the pressure from the Dutch, led the Company to pay greater attention to India. They also put out feelers in other parts of south-east Asia. The voyage of the *Globe* to the Bay of Bengal and the Gulf of Siam in 1611 resulted in the establishment of English factories in Ayuthia, then the capital of Siam, and at Patani on the east coast of the Malay peninsula. Between 1600 and 1612 twenty-six large ships sailed for the East, representing a total investment approaching £500,000. Exports of bullion and goods accounted for less than half of this amount; the rest was spent on the voyages. The average profit for the period was about 20 per cent a year.

Despite Dutch hostility, the East India Company during the first twenty years of its operations established quite a number of factories in south-east Asia. A review of those establishments in 1617 gave the following picture:

There were two factories at Achin and Tiku on the island of Sumatra at which it was possible to dispose of large quantities of

Indian goods in return for gold, camphor, pepper and benjamin. Then there was Bantam on the island of Java which was the major trading centre, importing Indian goods and exporting between 60,000 and 150,000 sacks of pepper a year. Nearby was Jaccatra, the modern Djakarta, which provided arrack, rice and fish for ships' provisions, but it was reported that a settlement there would be difficult because of the exorbitant sums demanded by the king for ground on which to build a factory. A settlement had recently been established at Jambi in Sumatra where Indian cloth was in demand and about 10,000 sacks of pepper could be obtained. At Patani on the Malay peninsula there was a market for Indian cloth, but there were few articles to export and trade was on the decline. Farther north, at Ayuthia in Siam, there was a market for Indian cloth in return for which gold, silver and deer skins could be obtained providing, as the report observed, "the country were in a state of peace". Sukadana on the island of Borneo held out promise of diamonds, bezoar stones and gold if this trade had not been ruined (it was sourly remarked) by the ignorance of the first factors. At Banjarmassin further east, similar produce was available but it was recommended that the factory should be withdrawn because the character of the natives was so treacherous. At Macassar there was a good potential market for Indian cloth in return for which it was reported that the best rice could be obtained. The snag was that this settlement, although abandoned by the Dutch, was visited by the Portuguese. Finally, at Banda there was also a considerable demand for Indian cloth in return for which about 1,000 tons of nutmegs and mace could be purchased and "a still greater quantity could peace be established between the Europeans trading to it".

A few years later, in 1623, the climax of the struggle between the English and the Dutch Companies was reached. The Dutch arrested ten members of the staff of the East India Company, alleging a conspiracy to seize the Dutch fort on the island of Amboina. They were tortured to extract confessions and put to death. The "massacre of Amboina" poisoned relations between England and Holland for half a century or more. Some compensation was afforded by the Treaty of Westminster in 1654 after the Anglo-Dutch war; but the East India Company was never able to re-establish its foothold.

The "massacre of Amboina" marks a turning-point in English

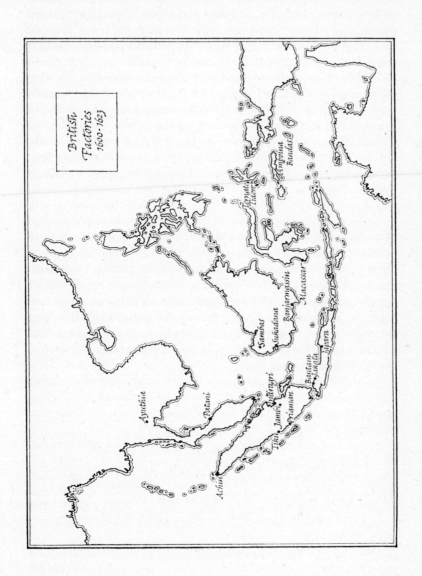

British
Factories
1600-1623

Ayuthia

Patani

Tiku
Jambi
Indragiri
Priaman
Bantam
Jacatra
Jupara
Macassar
Banjarmassin
Sukadana
Samboa
Ternate
Tidore
Amboyna
Banda I.

Achin

penetration of the East Indies. Thereafter, attempts to challenge the Dutch were abandoned and the number of English factories declined. The factory at Macassar continued in being until 1667 and the main depot remained at Bantam until 1682. But then the English were obliged to quit Java also, and were confined to their last remaining outpost of Bencoolen in Sumatra.

Yet, in spite of this withdrawal, English trade with the East Indies continued with profit. In the first sixty years of the Company only one expedition was a total failure because the ships were lost at sea. Apart from that, the returns were generally substantial. In fact, the English Company was paying higher dividends than the Dutch—who devoted some of their profits to strengthening their hold on the Indies by means of fortifications and fighting ships.

RETREAT

The repulse of the English in the Indies was an added inducement for them to turn their attention to other quarters, mainly to India itself but also to the countries nearby. There, they were on equal terms with the Dutch, and found enough trade in calicoes, indigo, saltpetre, coffee and pepper to satisfy them. In the longer run it was to prove more profitable than the trade in cloves and nutmegs, although it did not seem so at the time. English trading activities shifted from the islands of the Indies to the mainland—to Siam, Indo-China and Burma. Some factories were established, but they were short-lived.

There was a change of policy on the part of the Company. At first it had tried to collect cargoes by local trading, but this turned out to be unprofitable. The Asian traders were much better at it. The Company's servants also indulged in private enterprise as a means of supplementing their meagre salaries, with adverse effects on its commerce. In 1661 the Company, accepting the situation, withdrew from the port-to-port trade and concentrated its factories, thereby economizing on the number of staff required. The factories were supplied with local produce by "country ships" which were not controlled by the Company.

This was not the only change which occurred in the middle of the seventeenth century. Conflict with the Dutch once more brought about a shift of policy, and introduced strategic considerations where commercial considerations had predominated. There was no good harbour for naval repairs on the Coromandel coast of India during the period of the north-east monsoon, particularly the stormy period of October–November. During the first Anglo-Dutch war (1652–4) the Dutch had an advantage because they were able to operate from the port of Malacca which they had acquired from the Portuguese in 1641, whereas the English had no naval repair station on the eastern side of the Bay of Bengal.

The English involvement on that coast, however, arose neither from strategic considerations nor from direct trade interests. Rather it was the involuntary consequence of the position which the Company had established in India—and of the Company's gift to Siam in the shape of Phaulkon, a Greek adventurer. When Phaulkon arrived at Ayuthia in 1678 from the English factory at Bantam he was no longer in the Company's service; but he was employed by Company agents for their private trading ventures, and entered the Siamese service to further the interests of the English against the Dutch. His ability soon won him promotion to the post of Superintendent of Foreign Trade. Mergui was at this time a flourishing Siamese port trading with the Coromandel coast. The trade was in the hands of Indians, but Phaulkon aimed to develop it by means of ships flying the Siamese flag under the command of English "interlopers"—the Dutch word for those who traded without a licence. For that purpose he employed former Company servants such as Samuel White whom he appointed Superintendent of Mergui. Friction with the Indian traders followed, and White harried their shipping. His behaviour caused no little embarrassment to the English factory at Madras. In 1686 King James II issued a proclamation forbidding his subjects from serving in the ships of foreign rulers in the East; and two warships were sent from Madras to order the English to quit and to obtain compensation. The warships arrived at Mergui in 1687 and received compliance from the English, but failed to take precautions against the Siamese who launched a surprise attack, sank one of the ships and killed most of the English on shore.

At this juncture the French made their appearance on the scene. A French squadron was sent to Siam with the object of seizing Bangkok and Mergui. When the East India Company heard of this, it made representations to James II pointing out the seriousness of the position for its shipping in the Bay of Bengal if the French were to hold Mergui on the eastern side in addition to Pondicherry on the Coromandel coast. The King was impressed, and sent instructions to Madras for the seizure of Mergui before it fell into French hands. A frigate was despatched to reinforce the two warships, but arrived to find that the French had got there first and had to surrender. This was the ignominious end of the English attempt to take Mergui. Soon afterwards the Siamese turned against Phaulkon and the French, and by 1690 the foreigners had been cleared from the country.

Attention now shifted to Burma—to the port of Syriam from which Madras received cargoes of teak for shipbuilding. A frigate was sent there for repairs in 1689, and an approach was made to the Burmese court at Ava. The Burmese were responsive, and wanted an English factory to be opened at Syriam; but this was beyond the competence of Madras. A compromise was reached by the appointment of an English "Chief" who would take charge of an English dockyard at Syriam and be responsible for the English merchants trading in Burma; but this had to be an unofficial arrangement, for the Company could not be brought into it, and the English Chief consequently lacked authority. Later the position was formalized to some extent through the replacement of the Chief by a Resident who was given regular contracts by the Company for the construction and repair of ships. The French also began to display an interest in Syriam, and set up a dockyard there. But both the English and French dockyards were closed after 1740 when the Mons rebelled against the Burmese. The English factory was burnt by the Mons in 1743 and the Resident left.

Ten years later French attempts at penetration were resumed by a mission from Pondicherry to the Mons. The English at Madras became suspicious and reported that the French intended to seize Negrais. They urged the Company to forestall the French by planting a settlement there. This plan was approved and in 1753 an expedition sent from Madras took possession of the island. Ironically, the supposed French design which this move was intended to forestall had been rejected by the French Company. The alliance of the French with the Mons brought the English and Burmese together, and in 1757 the Burmese king, in return for military supplies, recognized the English settlement on Negrais. Simultaneously, however, the Company was issuing orders for a complete withdrawal from Burma. The Burmese success had eliminated the French threat, and with the Seven Years' War in progress all resources were needed to deal with the French in India. But British withdrawal from Burma was not a simple matter. The garrison was brought away from Negrais in 1759, but a small party was left behind to guard surplus stores. This party was surprised and massacred by Burmese troops commanded by a French officer. Thereafter relations between the Company and the Burmese ceased for a long span.

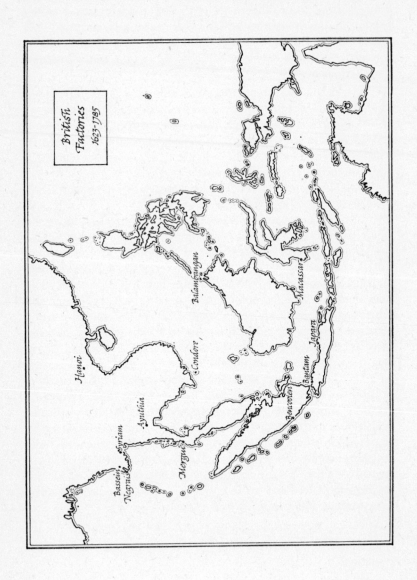

British Factories
1623-1785

Hanoi

Bassein
Negrais
Syriam
Ayuthia
Tenasserim
Condore
Bilanguangan
Macassar
Bencoolen
Bantam
Japara

2

RETURN

THE FIRST PHASE:
PENANG AND SINGAPORE

DURING the Seven Years' War the need was again felt for a British naval station on the eastern side of the Bay of Bengal, for the French were able to besiege Madras by land and sea without hindrance from British naval forces. Consequently, when the war ended the East India Company ordered a search for a port on the eastern side of the Bay.

Although strategic considerations were now dominant, commercial potentialities were not neglected. The spice trade still interested the Company. In addition, the trade between India and China had developed, Indian piece-goods and opium being traded for Chinese produce via Malaya and the Indies. Moreover, after Pitt's Commutation Act of 1784, which drastically reduced the duty on tea, imports of tea from China by the East India Company more than doubled. The importance of protecting this trade route increased correspondingly. So the most desirable objective was a repair station on the main sea route to China which would also serve as a trading centre for the Malay archipelago. Balambangan was tried, but the establishment was soon wiped out by pirates. In 1771 the Company instructed Madras to make inquiries about possibilities in Achin and Kedah. Francis Light, who captained a "country ship" trading between India and the Malay peninsula, was zealous in the promotion of this search. Rhio was investigated, but the Dutch had got there first. Light then recommended Junk-seylon, where he had settled as a private trader, and Penang which he had long had in view. Eventually in 1786 the Company decided on Penang. There was no intention of acquiring political control over Malaya. Pitt's India Act of 1784 had declared:

". . . schemes of conquest and extension of dominion . . . are measures repugnant to the wish, the honour and policy of this nation".

Francis Light negotiated the agreement with the Sultan of Kedah, which from the point of view of the Company was a simple

27

commercial transaction. In return for the cession of the island the Company undertook to pay the Sultan $6,000 a year. The Sultan also thought that he could count on British support against his enemies, but it transpired later that he could not. Meanwhile the establishment of Penang proceeded under Francis Light as superintendent in accordance with his instructions:

> "to secure a port of refreshment and repair for the King's, the Company's and the country ships, and we must leave it to time and your good management to establish it as a port of commerce".

The latter objective was to be promoted by making Penang a free port. It did not prosper, and for some time its future was in doubt. But in 1796, when England and France were again at war, Wellesley, the future Duke of Wellington, reported very strongly in favour of retaining the island:

> "It is a most desirable place to retain because scarcely a ship of the expedition has failed to sustain damage from the violence of the south-west monsoon . . . Such was the diligence of the governing power, and the capabilities of the place, that not less than 10,000 people in addition to the inhabitants were daily fed: above 6,000 of these Europeans . . . If it be a benefit to live under the Company's government, it cannot be expected that any man will spend his time and fortune upon a settlement which they intend to abandon; and as the settlement is, as I have above shown, of infinite advantage to the Company, and as it will undoubtedly be quitted by the settlers if the Company's government does not declare its intention of keeping it, it is recommended that it should make that declaration in the most explicit terms and adhere to it faithfully . . ."

In 1800 a strip of the mainland opposite the island—Province Wellesley—was acquired for a further $4,000 a year. Then the Admiralty decided to build a naval shipyard and arsenal at Penang. This induced the Company to take the plunge, and in 1804 Penang was promoted to the status of a Presidency—on a par with Bombay, Madras and Calcutta. It was as Assistant Secretary of this expensive station that in 1805 Thomas Raffles arrived at Penang.

Raffles at that time was not 25 years old. His father was a ship's captain in the West Indian trade. At the age of twelve he entered

28

a boarding-school at Hammersmith, but had to leave after two years because the family lacked the money for him to continue. Through the influence of his uncle he then got a job as a temporary clerk with the East India Company in Leadenhall Street. His father died and left him as the bread-winner for his mother and four sisters. It was fortunate for them that Raffles had an enormous capacity for work, matched by a driving ambition. In addition to the long hours which he spent at East India House, he gave some time each day to self-improvement and the completion of his interrupted education. It was typical of the man that he employed the months of the voyage to Penang in acquiring a working knowledge of Malay.

His interest in, and knowledge of, the people of the Malay archipelago was exceptional; but in other respects he was a child of his age. His liberalism was combined with undogmatic Christianity and adherence to free trade. Profit was not incompatible with principle. In respect of the opium trade in Java he observed :

> "while in the hands of the Company it would be the certain source of immense gain, at the same time that the cause of Humanity would be served by selling the least possible quantity of the poison for the greatest obtainable price . . ."

To sell as little as possible for the highest possible price is surely the dream of every profiteer. Recognizing that the commodity was "poison", he might have adopted an attitude akin to his position on the slave trade where he shared the views of his friend Wilberforce; but that would have put him too far ahead of his time. His interest in things Malay extended to the flora and fauna which he collected assiduously: he was the founder of the London Zoo. In the East he was the founder of much more.

Penang faced the problem of competition from Malacca, which had been in English hands since 1795. Napoleon's seizure of Holland was an invitation to the British to take the Dutch possessions in the East and hold them in trust until the end of the war. The restoration of Malacca to the Dutch, which Britain had promised, would mean the re-establishment of a rival. This danger was to be eliminated by the drastic method of destroying the fortifications and public buildings and transferring the merchants and their business to Penang.

Raffles, however, took a different view. Promoted to Secretary of the Penang Presidency in 1807, he visited Malacca and submitted

29

a report which recommended that the Company's policy towards Malacca be reversed. He argued that most of the inhabitants of Malacca, which had been in European hands since 1511, had a stake in the country and could not be induced to move, especially as their position at Penang would be less attractive. Moreover, the natives regarded Britain as pledged to protect them, for when the British took over Malacca they had been encouraged to remain. He analysed the position of Malacca in the carrying trade of the region, showing that this trade could not be switched to Penang. He also pointed to the usefulness of Malacca as a check on piracy. Then he reached the core of his argument:

". . . although the present fortifications and public works of every description may be effectually destroyed, the possession of Malacca will ever be a most desirable object to a European power and to our enemy. Prince of Wales Island (Penang) has by no means the same advantage and command within the Straits that Malacca possesses. Every ship that passes up or down must be observed from the latter place, and should this station ever be held by an enterprising enemy, not only Penang but our more important China trade would be materially endangered. We have now the command. Why give it up unless we are forced?"

Furthermore, if it were handed back to the Dutch they would make it a free port and so cripple the trade of Penang; but if it were retained there could be no problem of rivalry or competition. Concluding, Raffles looked still further afield, giving an insight into his later policies:

"With the assistance of Malacca the whole of the Malay Rajahs in the Straits and to the Eastward might be rendered not only subservient but, if necessary, tributary."

At this stage, however, his views prevailed only so far as to obtain from the Governor-General an interim suspension of the withdrawal from Malacca.

Raffles's horizon continued to expand. In 1810 the prospect of his appointment to take charge of the recently captured Moluccas provided the occasion for him to visit Calcutta for an interview with the Governor-General, Lord Minto:

"I found that, though the appointment to the Moluccas had not actually taken place, it was promised to another. I, in conse-

quence, relinquished all idea of it, and at once drew his Lordship's attention to Java, by observing that there were other
islands worthy of his Lordship's consideration besides the
Moluccas; Java for instance. On the mention of Java, his Lordship cast a look of such scrutiny, anticipation and kindness upon
me as I shall never forget. 'Yes,' said he, 'Java is an interesting
island; I shall be happy to receive any information you can give
me concerning it.' This was enough to encourage me; and from
this moment all my views, all my plans, and all my mind were
devoted to create such an interest regarding Java as should lead
to its annexation to our Eastern Empire . . ."

While Raffles thought in terms of annexation, the East India
Company took a more limited view. The Company agreed to an
expedition against Java, but Lord Minto warned Raffles:

"I must tell you in confidence that I have received the sanction
of government at home for this expedition, but that the views of
the Directors do not go beyond the expulsion or reduction of
the Dutch power, the destruction of their fortifications, the distribution of their arms and stores to the natives, and the evacuation of the island by our own troops."

However, on Raffles's own suggestion Minto sent him to Malacca
to gather information for the expedition and to enter into relations
with the native chiefs. From that advance post he sent a series of
reports to Lord Minto. Much of his reporting was on an elevated
plane:

"We may with great facility and without much trouble employ
our influence and mediation to heal the dissensions of the native
prices, to establish firmly ancient authorities, check innovations,
and prevent civil wars as much as lies in our power . . ."

So far so good: a conservative policy, no doubt, but altruistic. Then
comes a glimpse of the cloven hoof:

"The increase of security in the country will produce the increase
of both wealth and population which will of course cause an
increase in the consumption of opium, piece goods and other
Indian commodities."

He made an ingenious suggestion drawn from his study of the
history of the archipelago. Recalling how the ruler of the empire

of Majapahit in Java had held the title of Bitara or Lord Pro-
tector *vis-à-vis* some of the Malay states, he proposed that the
Governor-General of India should, with the consent of such states
as were willing, assume the title and role of Bitara. "This would
give a general right of superintendence over, and interference with,
all the Malay states . . ."

In 1811 the British expedition, with the Governor-General himself on board, sailed from Malacca for Java. *En route* the fleet
passed Singapore island, affording its ruler, the Temenggong, a
view of a concentration of sea-power greater than anything previously seen in those waters. The expedition sailed on through the
Karimata straits, previously thought to be unnavigable until Raffles
insisted on a reconnaissance. The defeat of the Dutch and the
occupation of Java were accomplished without much difficulty. It
proved more difficult to extricate the British, for Minto now took a
similar view to Raffles about the Company's instructions to evacuate.
He wrote to the President of the India Board of Control:

"I consider the main point as ascertained, and that Java will
supply resources at the least for its own expenses . . . It is now
most flourishing; but the field for improvement is inexhaustible.
All that I fear is the general peace . . . This ought not surely to
prevent us from beginning to perform the first duty of governments in improving the condition of the people that has become
tributary to our authority and tributary to our prosperity . . . The
exclusion of European masters from Java is impossible in the
present state of things. To make them richer, happier and to
give the people itself a feeling of independence which they are
now totally without would be the best receipt for making their
country less accessible to European invaders. But in our own
times this cannot be looked to, and the Government we have
established must instantly be replaced by the French whenever it
is withdrawn . . . I think we ought to make it an English colony
as soon as we can by the introduction of English colonists, English capital and therefore an English interest."

Minto had no illusion about the likelihood of the Company
adopting his policy. He recognized that the British were in Java
only temporarily. To Raffles, whom he left behind as Lieutenant-
General, his parting words were ". . . while we are here, let us do
all the good we can."

The Company's view was unaltered. Now that the threat from Java to the India and China trade had been removed, it was content and had no desire to be saddled with a large chunk of territory which was likely to prove a financial liability. It had much experience of the expansionist proclivities of its proconsuls, and was less impressed than Minto by the rosy picture painted by Raffles. If the Dutch could not make Java pay, the Company doubted whether Raffles could. But Minto was in charge and on the spot, and the Company could not but acquiesce, although with reluctance. The impulse for imperial expansion was much stronger at the periphery than at the centre.

Although Minto had assured the Company of the economic potentialities of Java, the first fruits of the occupation were a succession of deficits. In part these were due to the cost of military operations, deemed necessary to establish the British position. But the reforms introduced by Raffles in land tenure and revenue collection, which might have proved lucrative in the long run, did not help in the short term. Minto argued that a surplus from Java should be a secondary consideration, since if it had remained in the hands of the enemy it would have damaged the Company's trade and caused military expenditure. But the Company did not see it in that light.

If the Company was disappointed, Raffles was undeterred and eager to extend British influence further:

"The great island of Borneo, the Sooloo Island, Linghen (Lingga) and Rhio, Bali, the East coast of Sumatra, Siam, Gambodia (Cambodia), Cochin China, etc. are free from all connexion with the former ruling power in these seas and want but the attention of our enlightened and liberal Government to add extensively to the commerce of India and to the permanent political ascendancy of the British influence in these seas."

But from the Governor-General of India came a reasoned and damping reply. If Java and the Moluccas were to be restored to the Dutch any British settlements established in their neighbourhood would be regarded with hostility. There would be continual disputes, and there might be conflict. If the formation of British settlements would not be contemplated when the Dutch had resumed control of Java, how could it be just or expedient to attempt it while the British were temporarily in charge? Moreover,

Parliament had prohibited the East India Company from acquiring territory south of the equator.

The defeat of Napoleon was depressing news for Raffles. The Hundred Days revived his hopes:

> "The wonderful and extraordinary change in the politics of Europe by the reappearance of Buonaparte has with all its horrors showed one consoling ray on this sacred Isle; and Java may yet be permanently English."

But his hopes were dashed: the British Government agreed to restore the Dutch possessions in the East. In 1816 Raffles left Java under a cloud and returned home.

In England Raffles was cleared of charges of misconduct. Although the Company still regarded some of his policies as unwise, he was knighted for his services. He accepted the appointment to take charge of Bencoolen, now the only surviving East India Company station in the Indies, and was given the rank of Lieutenant-Governor. Almost as soon as he arrived back in the Indies, in 1818, he resumed his theme of Britain's position in the East:

> "The Dutch possess the only passes through which ships must sail into the Archipelago, the Straits of Sunda and Malacca; and the British have now not an inch of ground to stand upon between the Cape of Good Hope and China, nor a single friendly post at which they can water and obtain refreshments." [There was no harbour at Bencoolen.] ". . . To effect the objects contemplated some convenient station within the Archipelago is necessary; both Bencoolen and Prince of Wales Island are too far removed, and unless we succeed in obtaining a position in the Straits of Sunda we have no alternative but to fix it in the most advantageous position we can find within the Archipelago; this would be somewhere in the neighbourhood of Bintang."

Bintang lies some twenty miles from Singapore.

At first Raffles attempted to expand in Sumatra—north to Padang, south to the Straits of Sunda and inland towards Palembang—but at each turn he was blocked by the Dutch. So he paid a visit to Calcutta to see Lord Hastings who had succeeded Lord Minto as Governor-General. His mission was successful. He received authority to secure the free passage of the Straits of Malacca, as "an object of essential importance to our political and commercial interests", by establishing stations at Achin and Rhio. There was one reservation, very needful for Raffles:

"It is expressly to be understood . . . that the object in fixing upon a Post of this nature is not the extension of any territorial influence, but strictly limited to the occupation of an advantageous position for the protection of our commerce."

The Dutch perceived that something was afoot and took steps to anticipate the English at Rhio which they claimed to control as a dependency of their government at Malacca. This contingency had been foreseen, and Raffles was instructed to examine the possibility of an arrangement with the Sultan of Johore. In December, 1818, Raffles sailed from Calcutta, and wrote a few days later:

"We are now on our way to the Eastward, in the hope of doing something, but I much fear the Dutch have hardly left us an inch of ground to stand upon. My attention is principally turned to Johore, and you must not be surprised if my next letter to you is dated from the site of the ancient city of Singapura."

Meanwhile, the Dutch were making representations in London about the activities of Raffles and found a sympathetic hearing. Castlereagh informed them that both he and Canning disapproved of the political adventures of Raffles. The India Board of Control was requested to bring him into line. The Board passed on this censure to the East India Company, and the Court of Directors wrote to the Governor-General saying that Raffles had overstepped the limits of his authority and suggesting that he should be replaced. But three months before this letter left London Raffles had hoisted the Union Jack on Singapore.

When the British arrived at Singapore the island was inhabited by some 500 Malays, most of them seafarers living in their boats, and a number of Chinese settled inland and working on gambier plantations. The sovereignty of the island was confused and contested. The immediate ruler was the Temenggong, but he was subject to the Sultan of Johore and the Sultanate was in dispute between two brothers. Raffles installed the more amenable of the two contenders as Sultan, and concluded a treaty with him on February 6, 1819, which is regarded as the date of the foundation of Singapore.

In the treaty Raffles agreed that the Company would pay the Sultan $3,000 a year and would extend British protection, in return for which the Company would be entitled to establish a factory and have control of the port. It would have been much cheaper a century before. Captain Alexander Hamilton, an earlier voyager to the East, recorded:

> "In anno 1703 I called at Johore on my way to China and he (the prince of Johore) treated me very kindly and made me a present of the island of Singapore; but I told him it could be of no use to a private person, though a proper place for a company to settle a colony on . . ."

Raffles's action received a cautious endorsement from the Governor-General:

> ". . . your engagements with the presumed legitimate Chief of Johor and the local government of Singapoor are provisionally confirmed . . . It is intended to maintain the post of Singapoor for the present."

But Raffles as usual was running well ahead of this provisional policy:

> "Our eventual object is of course to secure the independence of Bornean, Sumatran and other States with which we have been in alliance for the last seventy years, and further if practicable to regain the Settlements of Malacca, Padang and Banca . . . Our object is not territory but Trade; a great commercial emporium and a fulcrum whence we may extend our influence politically as circumstances may hereafter require. By taking immediate possession we put a negative to the Dutch claim of exclusion and at the same time revive the drooping confidence of our Allies and friends. One free port in these seas must eventually destroy the spell of Dutch monopoly; and what Malta is in the West, that may Singapore become in the East . . ."

In London the news of the acquisition of Singapore was received as another of Raffles's deplorable escapades. The British Government was on the point of entering into negotiations with the Dutch Government for an amicable arrangement. That project was nipped in the bud. Instead there was the prospect that, should the Dutch expel the Singapore garrison by force, Britain would either have to submit or to demand reparation which might lead to war. Nevertheless, in dealings with the Dutch the British Government took a firm stand. Castlereagh instructed the British ambassador at The Hague:

> "There are two principles from which the British Government can under no circumstances be expected to depart; the one is, they cannot acquiesce in a practical exclusion or in a mere permissive of British commerce throughout the immense extent of the Eastern Archipelago; nor can they consent so far to expose the direct Commerce of this Country with China to all the obvious dangers and disadvantages which would result, especially in time of war, from all the military and naval keys of the Straits of Malacca being exclusively in the hands of the Netherlands Government."

This argument was reinforced by the consideration that the duty on China tea provided about one-tenth of the total revenue of the British exchequer.

The negotiations between the British and Dutch Governments were protracted. The longer they went on, the more the new settlement flourished and the more unlikely it became that the Dutch would take drastic action or that the British would quit. Fifteen months after the founding of the post the population was approaching 5,000. The volume of trade soon surpassed that of Malacca. A constitution and code of laws for the settlement were drafted and promulgated under the supervision of Raffles and steps were taken towards the foundation of the college that he had long envisaged.

Raffles left the Indies for the last time in 1824. In the same year an agreement was reached by which the Dutch ceded to the British their possessions in continental India together with Malacca and Singapore, while the British disclaimed all interest in the East Indian archipelago which meant withdrawal from Bencoolen. It was an arrangement which Raffles approved, although it fell far short of his ambitions. But he had put his foot in the gateway of the East.

BURMA

The establishment of the British position on the Malay peninsula was partly the result of interest in trade, partly for the protection of shipping, and mainly for strategic reasons; but it was also due in no

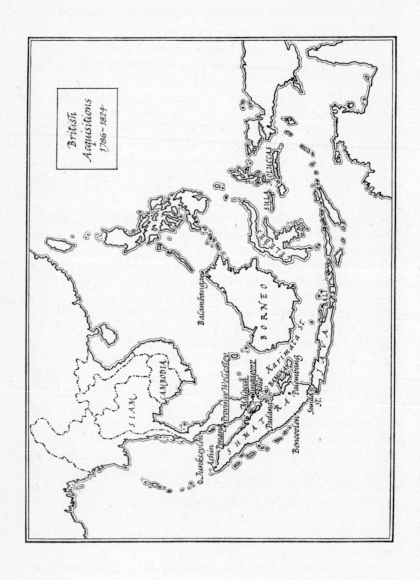

British Acquisitions 1786–1824

small measure to the enterprise of the Company's servants in creating situations from which the Company had not the will or the inclination to withdraw. In Burma a different set of motives was operative. Here it might be said that a large empire was the best reason for a larger empire, for British expansion into Burma was primarily determined by its proximity to India.

After the "massacre of Negrais" relations with Burma were allowed to lapse, although the Burmese requested and strongly desired their continuance. As the British extended their hold in India and the Burmese conquered the Arakan they found themselves neighbours on the Arakan-Bengal frontier. When Arakanese refugees were pursued over that frontier by the Burmese the Governor-General was led to consider the re-opening of relations with Burma. Captain Symes was sent as envoy to Ava in 1795 and was given three tasks: to settle the Arakan frontier incident, to persuade the Burmese to close their ports to French warships, and to negotiate a commercial treaty allowing an agent of the Company to reside at Rangoon. Times had changed and so had the Company's attitude. Symes recorded his own view of the importance of Burma:

"British India is more deeply concerned in her commerce and connexion with that part of the Burman empire called Pegue than many persons, in other respects intimately versed in the affairs of India, seem to be aware. This interest points to three distinct objects: first to secure from that quarter regular supplies of timber for shipbuilding, without which the British marine of India could exist but on a very contracted scale; secondly, to introduce into that country as much of our manufactures as its consumption may require, and to endeavour to find a mart in the South-west dominions of China by means of the great river of Ava; thirdly, to guard with vigilance against every encroachment or advance which may be made by foreign nations to divert the trade into other channels, and obtain a permanent settlement in a country contiguous to the capital of our possessions. This last consideration supersedes all others in the magnitude of the consequences that might ultimately result from it."

The Burmese refused to exclude the French but agreed to admit the British, and in the following year Captain Cox arrived in Rangoon as British Resident. He was not a success and had to be recalled after two years.

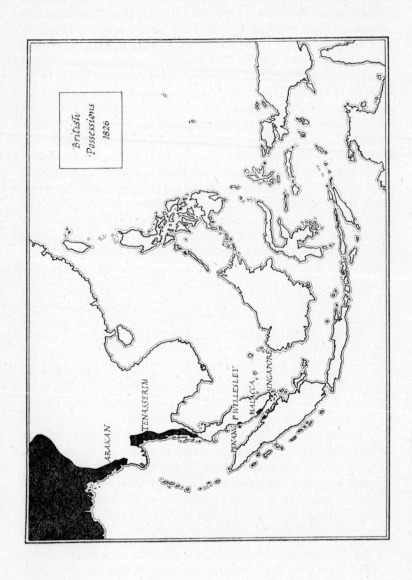

British
Possessions
1826

ARAKAN

TENASSERIM

PENANG P WELLESLEY

MALACCA

SINGAPORE

Another outbreak of revolt in Arakan and a fresh influx of refugees created a repetition of the previous friction. The Burmese demanded the expulsion of the refugees; the British declined; the Burmese threatened invasion. In 1802 Symes was despatched on his second mission to Ava to deal with this threat. His patience was rewarded by an abatement of the Burmese demands and permission to re-establish a British Resident at Rangoon. The Resident did not stay long but the Arakan frontier was quiet for a while, although similar incidents recurred later.

Eventually the confrontation between Burmese and British imperialism occurred. When the Burmese thrust into Assam and Manipur, the Government of India began to worry about the safety of Bengal. The British tried to call a halt, declaring a protectorate over the state of Cachar, but in 1824 the Burmese invaded and were preparing to attack Chittagong. The British declared war first and captured Rangoon by a seaborne expedition. After a series of British successes the Burmese were obliged to treat for peace, and accepted the terms laid down by the British in the Treaty of Yandabo in 1826. The terms were the cession of Arakan, Tenasserim, Assam and Manipur plus an indemnity equivalent to £1 million, an undertaking not to interfere in the states on the north-east frontier of British India, the reception of a British Resident at Amarapura and the despatch of a Burmese envoy to Calcutta. Burma lost two large coastal provinces. Arakan was ceded "to prevent all future disputes respecting the boundary between the two great nations", but for the acquisition of Tenasserim no reason was given.

SIAM

The missing motive is to be found in the development of British relations with Siam. Raffles had complained to Lord Minto in 1811 of the "slavish and humiliating manner, by no means accommodated to the habits of Englishmen", in which trade with Siam had to be carried on:

> "On arriving in port the most valuable part of the cargo is immediately presented to the king, who takes as much as he pleases; the remaining part is chiefly consumed in presents to the courtiers and other great men, while the refuse of the cargo is then permitted to be exposed to sale. The part which is consumed in presents to the great men is entire loss: for that which the king receives

he generally returns a present which is seldom adequate to the value of the goods which he has received; but by dint of begging and repeated solicitation this is sometimes increased a little."

More important than these irritants, however, were the facts of geography. Just as expansion in India had brought the East India Company into conflict with the Burmese, so the acquisition of footholds on the Malay peninsula involved it in encounters with Siam.

In 1821 the Siamese asserted their suzerainty over Kedah by an invasion of that state. Whatever the Sultan of Kedah may have understood by the agreement with the Company for the cession of Penang, no help was forthcoming from that quarter. Yet the Company could not remain indifferent. The Sultan himself took refuge in Penang, and refugees poured into Province Wellesley where they were under British protection. This crisis, together with growing concern for trade with Siam, led to the despatch of a mission to Bangkok, without result.

A fresh attempt was made when the Anglo-Burmese war began. Envoys were sent from Penang to enlist the help of the Raja of Ligor; but they found that the Raja was only a Siamese official, and the Siamese were more interested in their own ambitions in the Malay states than in the British involvement in Burma. The Governor of Penang urged Calcutta to restore the Sultan of Kedah and extend British protection over the Malay states threatened by Siam, but the Government of India had no desire to add to its commitments at that juncture. Captain Burney, a nephew of Fanny Burney, who had been military secretary to the Governor of Penang, was chosen to go as envoy to Bangkok with the object of assuring the Siamese Government that the British conquest of Tenasserim was in no way a threat to Siam and that the Company had no intention of extending its hold over the Malay peninsula.

The Government of India originally intended to do a deal with Siam at the expense of Burma. They thought that they might be able to restore the Sultan of Kedah and obtain a commercial treaty from Siam in return for part of the Tenasserim coast which they intended to acquire from Burma. The Company did not want to hold on to that territory and thought that Siam might be interested, especially as the area had once been under Siamese rule. But by the time that Burney was despatched on his mission to Bangkok the Government of India had second thoughts. In part this was due to a feeling that they could not hand over the Burmese to the harsh treatment that they would undoubtedly receive at the hands of the Siamese. But the change of heart was also due to a revised appreciation of the strategic importance of the Tenasserim coast. The French had maintained a naval base there in the previous century and the location was useful for any operations that might be required against Burma or Siam.

Burney succeeded in negotiating a treaty only at the price of some obscurity in its provisions. The object of his mission, apart from improving the terms of trading, was to secure the maximum independence of the states of Kedah, Perak, Trengganu and Kelantan without British commitment. In the case of Kedah the Siamese would not budge, and the British had to remove the ex-Sultan from Penang to the more remote Malacca. The position of Perak was obscure in the Burney treaty, but Captain Low, an agent of the Penang Government, soon afterwards negotiated an alliance with the Sultan of Perak. If this alliance did not conflict with the Burney treaty, it hardly corresponded to the assurances given to the Siamese; but the alliance was not repudiated by the Company and came to be regarded as valid. Perak therefore acquired British protection. But the position of Trengganu and Kelantan remained obscure and later became critical.

BORNEO

As so often, the British were finding that their presence in the Malay peninsula could not be static: they were obliged by circumstances and the zeal of their subordinates to extend their influence. One perennial motive for that expansion was the establishment and maintenance of law and order. None gave it more occasion for exercise than the pirates of the Eastern seas—the Lanun, Balanini and other seafaring tribes. The very prosperity of Singapore and the afflux of shipping provided a magnet, and in 1837 the Government of India was impelled to station a naval force in the Straits to cope with them. An important component of this force was the first steamship to be sent to that area, the *Diana*, which alone could deal effectively with the pirate *prahus*, for sailing vessels could be outmanoeuvred by the use of oars.

Two years later came a new weapon against the pirates in the person of James Brooke. It is somewhat ironical that the most drastic measures against piracy were to be taken by an English freebooter. He was the son of a Bengal civil servant and had served in the Anglo-Burmese war in Assam where he was wounded. He left the Company's service, and when his father died he invested his inheritance in a yacht, the *Royalist*, and arrived in Borneo to explore and research. Not for nothing was he a disciple of Raffles. Like his mentor, he believed that commercial prosperity demanded territorial possession: without it a mere commercial settlement could not succeed. Like Raffles too, he had the welfare of the natives at heart: he believed that government "must be directed to the advancement of the native interests and the development of native resources, rather than by a flood of European colonization to aim at possession only, without reference to the indefeasible rights of the Aborigines". He found the region of Sarawak in revolt against the Sultan of Brunei, and in return for his help in putting down the rebellion he was given the governorship of Sarawak in 1841. As Governor he introduced law and order, including strong measures against piracy. At the same time he tried to interest the British Government in Brunei. The development of the steamship suggested the need for a coaling station between Singapore and Hong Kong (which was acquired in 1841), and both Brunei and the island of Labuan possessed seams of coal.

Brooke's enthusiasm for the suppression of piracy was less than welcome to the Sultan of Brunei whose revenues were adversely affected. In 1846 he turned against Brooke and tried to have him assassinated. The plot failed, and with the help of the Navy's China squadron Brooke captured Brunei. The Sultan fled, but was allowed to return on promise of good behaviour. As a token Sarawak was ceded in full sovereignty to Brooke. At the same time Palmerston as Foreign Secretary authorized the acceptance of the offer of Labuan made by the Sultan and of a commercial treaty, and the agreement was concluded in 1846. Brooke returned to England, was duly knighted and appointed Governor of Labuan. This was very respectable progress in the space of seven years. The Dutch tried to protest that this expansion was in contravention of the Anglo-Dutch treaty of 1824, but got short shrift from Palmerston.

THE SECOND PHASE:
CONQUEST OF BURMA

Meanwhile relations with Burma did not prosper: this was hardly surprising after the treaty of Yandabo. The life of the British Resi-

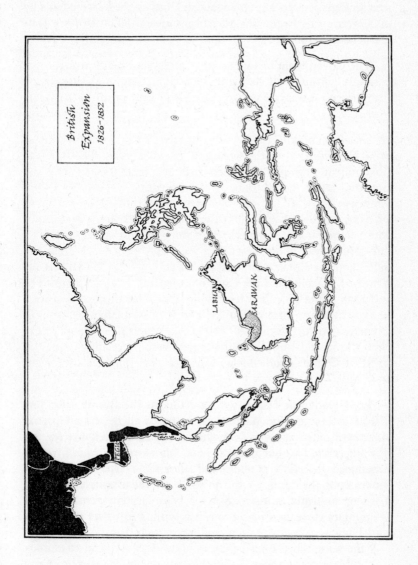

British
Expansion
1826-1852

LABUAN

SARAWAK

PEGU

dent was made uncomfortable, and in 1840 he was withdrawn. There were frequent complaints of ill-treatment from British subjects in Rangoon. In 1851 two British ships' captains were fined by the Governor of Pegu. The Governor-General of India, Lord Dalhousie, decided to act :

> "The Government of India could never, consistently with its own safety, permit itself to stand for a single day in an attitude of inferiority towards a native power, and least of all to the Court of Ava."

He sent Commodore Lambert in command of two warships to demand the dismissal of the Governor and reparation. The Burmese Government promptly complied with the first demand, and the Governor was replaced. But when a deputation was sent to discuss compensation with his successor they were refused admission in what they regarded as an insulting manner. Whereupon Commodore Lambert declared a blockade of the port, and seized the King's ship which was lying there. The Burmese opened fire from the shore, and the Commodore responded with a will. "So all that fat is in the fire," observed the Governor-General: "We can't afford to be shown to the door anywhere in the East." He proceeded to send an expeditionary force to Rangoon with an ultimatum demanding compensation to the tune of £100,000. When the ultimatum expired the second Burmese war began. These proceedings were the target of Cobden's indictment in his tract on "How Wars are got up in India" :

> "Lord Dalhousie begins with a claim on the Burmese for less than a thousand pounds; which is followed by the additional demand of an apology from the Governor of Rangoon for the insult offered to our officers; next, his terms are raised to one hundred thousand pounds, and an apology from the King's ministers; then follows the invasion of the Burmese territory; when, suddenly, all demands for pecuniary compensation and apologies cease, and his Lordship is willing to accept the cession of Pegu as a 'compensation' and 'reparation' for the past, whilst at the same time he pens long minutes to prove how calamitous it will be to us to annex that province to our Indian empire! Conceding, I say, the *bona fides* of all this—ought not we to advertise in *The Times* for a Governor-General who can collect a debt of

a thousand pounds without annexing a territory which will be ruinous to our finances?"

But Cobden recognized that his was a minority view:

"Public opinion in this country has not hitherto been opposed to an extension of our dominion in the East. On the contrary, it is believed to be profitable to the nation, and all classes are ready to hail with approbation every fresh acquisition of territory, and to reward those conquerors who bring us home title-deeds, no matter, I fear, how obtained, to new Colonial possessions."

The upshot was that the province of Pegu, lying between Arakan and Tenasserim, was annexed by Britain in 1852, depriving Burma of all outlet to the sea. The Burmese Government had to submit, but refused to recognize this annexation.

It has been denied that the British motive for expansion in Burma was economic: the spread of civilization and of the Gospel was an argument used at the time. Yet economic considerations were undoubtedly present. Only three years after the annexation, a mission was sent to the Government of Burma with a view to developing trade along the route from Bhamo to Yunnan; but the Burmese, not unnaturally, were suspicious of the extension of British influence. When Arakan, Pegu and Tenasserim were formed into the province of British Burma in 1862 another mission was sent to Mandalay and succeeded in obtaining a commercial treaty and the stationing of a British agent there. There was keen competition between Britain, France and America for the China trade, and there was strong commercial pressure in London and in Rangoon for opening an overland route to China. This was an important motive for British expansion northward which led to the third Anglo-Burmese war. Another element in Anglo-Burmese relations was the British reaction to the bloodthirsty régime of King Thibaw, who began his reign by slaughtering his rivals.

The "Shoe Question" also played its part in generating friction. British envoys had long objected to having to take off their shoes as the Burmese did at royal audiences. In 1875 the Government of India instructed the British Resident in Mandalay that in future he was not to take off his shoes—which meant that thereafter he was not received in audience, and Anglo-Burmese relations suffered.

The determining factor, however, which led to war was the attempt of King Thibaw to call in the French. He sent a mission to Paris in 1883 and granted the French a number of concessions, which the French were obliged to forgo in the face of British opposition. Believing that a French syndicate would be ready to take over the timber industry from the Bombay Burmah Trading Corporation, the Burmese imposed a heavy fine upon the company. The case was a poor one, no doubt a false one, and the British Government asked the Burmese Court to submit the matter to an arbitrator appointed by the Viceroy of India. This request was ignored. The Viceroy, with approval from London, then issued an ultimatum demanding the acceptance of a British Resident at Mandalay with guard and steamer, and direct access to the King with shoes on; submission of Burma's external relations to the control of the Government of India; and proper facilities for British trade with China via Bhamo. This was a demand for the establishment of a British protectorate. The King replied that "friendly relations with France, Italy and other states have been, are being, and will be maintained". To a later generation this reply seems unexceptionable. At that time, however, it was taken as a challenge and a rejection of the British ultimatum. British forces crossed the border and within a fortnight Mandalay had fallen and King Thibaw had been taken captive. This was the end of the Burmese dynasty.

Having conquered the remainder of Burma the problem was what to do with it. There were not lacking those who had a very clear and distinct idea on this subject: for example, the London Chamber of Commerce presented a petition to Lord Randolph Churchill, Secretary of State for India, urging the immediate annexation of northern Burma or the establishment of a protectorate over that province. There was talk of "driving the iron horse" from India up the Irrawaddy to the gates of China. On January 1, 1886, the Viceroy declared that King Thibaw's territories had become part of the British Dominions. This decision was taken by the Conservative Government which was shortly to be replaced by a Liberal administration under Mr. Gladstone. There was sharp argument about the decision, but the difficulty of finding a replacement for Thibaw reinforced the *fait accompli* bequeathed by Lord Randolph Churchill. The Liberal Prime Minister argued that the war had been, in reality and in intention, a defensive war and confirmed the

annexation of northern Burma. So the whole of Burma was added
to the Indian Empire.

EXPANSION IN MALAYA

In Malaya too British control was extended, although the first
phase was one of consolidation. In a fit of optimism the three
settlements of Penang, Malacca and Singapore were combined to
form a Presidency of India. This was soon seen to be an over-
estimate and in 1829 the Straits Settlements were demoted to the
status of an appendage of the Government of Bengal until in 1851
they were transferred to the control of the Government of India.
Taking them all together they prospered; but they had grievances,
and in 1857 the European population, who numbered less than a
thousand in Singapore at this time, began to agitate for the ending
of control from India and the substitution of a government directly
responsible to the Crown.

They presented a petition to Parliament in which they complained that the Straits Settlements were too far from India for
their needs to be understood and met, and that since the Indian
Government no longer had a monopoly of trade with China it had
ceased to be much interested in the Straits; that the Settlements
were made to pay for the keep of convicts and also for the maintenance of an excessive quantity of troops, and yet there was no
council of any kind through which the European community could
make representations; that in the neighbouring Malay States also
British interests had suffered because of the neglect of the Indian
Government while their foreign competitors had made rapid progress.

This agitation was successful after a decade and in 1867 the
Straits Settlements were removed from the control of the Government of India and became a Crown Colony. The immediate result
of this was to make the control of the Straits even more remote.
In 1867, before the opening of the Suez Canal, the journey between
London and Singapore took 116 days. But communications developed very rapidly. The Canal, opened in 1869, reduced the time
of the journey to forty-two days. Freight and cargoes were increasingly carried by steamship and a telegraph link to Singapore was
established in 1870.

These developments put the Straits in closer touch with London
and in so doing removed one of the grievances about which the

D
49

local trading community had complained. But they had the unforeseen consequence of creating another cause for complaint. As it was so much easier to communicate with Singapore it was possible to bypass the London export agencies and deal directly with the area. Straits traders were also hit by the erection of tariffs round Indonesia and the Philippines. Both of these developments led to demands for the opening of fresh fields for economic activities in Malaya. Arguments were adduced for British intervention in the Malay States on the grounds that the disorders that were rife were damaging the trade of the Straits Settlements, endangering the capital invested from the Settlements in Malayan tin-mining and other enterprises, and impeding the further development of the peninsula. At this stage, however, the British Government was opposed to involvement in the Malay States. The Singapore Chamber of Commerce was informed in 1872:

". . . it is the policy of H.M.G. not to interfere in the affairs of the Malay States unless where it becomes necessary for the suppression of piracy or the punishment of aggression on our people or territories; and that if traders, prompted by the prospect of large gains, choose to run the risk of placing their persons and properties in the jeopardy which they are aware attends them in these countries under present circumstances, it is impossible for Government to be answerable for their protection or that of their property."

Between this year and the next came the change: it is not often that a shift of policy can be fixed so precisely. With the appointment of Sir Andrew Clarke as Governor of the Straits Settlements in 1873 came fresh instructions from Gladstone's Colonial Secretary, Lord Kimberley, who had hitherto been firmly opposed to the intervention:

"H.M.G. have, it need hardly be said, no desire to interfere in the internal affairs of the Malay States. But looking to the long and intimate connexion between them and the British Government, and to the well-being of the British Settlements themselves, H.M.G. find it incumbent upon them to employ such influence as they possess with the native Princes to rescue, if possible, those fertile and productive countries from the ruin which must befall them if the present disorders continue unchecked. I

50

have to request that you will carefully ascertain, as far as you are able, the actual condition of affairs in each State, and that you will report to me whether there are, in your opinion, any steps which can properly be taken by the Colonial Government to promote the restoration of peace and order, and to secure protection to trade and commerce with the native territories. I should wish you especially to consider whether it would be advisable to appoint a British Officer to reside in any of the States. Such an appointment could, of course, only be made with the full consent of the Native Government, and the expenses connected with it would have to be defrayed by the Government of the Straits Settlements."

Ostensibly the change came about in response to the complaint from Chinese merchants in the Straits Settlements. Hitherto British expansion in Malaya had been largely inspired by the unauthorized initiative of British proconsuls. In this instance it appeared to have been stimulated by Chinese traders. In fact, however, the reason for the change of heart by the British Government lay much deeper. Basically it was due to fear of foreign intervention. Before the instructions were issued to the new Governor of the Straits Settlements the Colonial Secretary had written to the Prime Minister:

"The condition of the Malay Peninsula is becoming very serious. It is the old story of misgovernment of Asiatic States. This might go on without any very serious consequence, except the stoppage of trade, were it not that the European and Chinese capitalists, stimulated by the great riches in tin mines which exist in some of the Malay States, are suggesting to the native princes that they should seek the aid of Europeans to enable them to put down the disorders which prevail. We are the paramount power on the Peninsula up to the limit of the States tributary to Siam, and, looking to the vicinity of India and our whole position in the East, I apprehend that it would be a serious matter if any other European power were to obtain a footing in the Peninsula."[1]

Strategy rather than trade was the determining factor.

The first step in implementing the new policy was the conclusion of the Pangkor engagement in 1874 with the State of Perak. This agreement confirmed the cession to Britain of some additional territory and also contained these two clauses:

[1] C. D. Cowan: *Nineteenth Century Malaya* p. 169.

"That the Sultan receive and provide a suitable residence for a British Officer who shall be accredited to his Court and whose advice must be asked and acted upon in all questions other than those touching Malay religion and custom.

"That the collection and control of all revenues and the general administration of the country be regulated under the advice of these Residents."

Even granted the fresh instructions which the new Governor had brought with him this was going rather far, as the Governor recognized. He admitted in his report to London that he had acted beyond his instructions; but the Colonial Secretary of the new Conservative Government let it pass without censure. The introduction of the system was inauspicious. The first British Resident was murdered at the instance of the Sultan whom he was sent to advise, necessitating a punitive military expedition. The installation of a British Resident at Sungei Ujong also required a military operation. In Selangor, however, things were better managed and there was no trouble. Experience of these first appointments led the Government to issue fresh instructions for the conduct of Residents in 1876:

"The Residents are not to interfere more frequently or to a greater extent than is necessary with the minor details of government; but their special objects should be the maintenance of peace and law, the initiation of a sound system of taxation, with the consequent development of the resources of the country, and the supervision of the collection of the revenue, so as to ensure the receipt of funds necessary to carry out the principal engagements of the Government, and to pay for the cost of the British officers and whatever establishments may be necessary to support them."

The Malay States were not only to be given British administration: they were also to be made to pay for it. The process continued: in 1888 the State of Pahang was obliged to accept a Resident after a British subject, a Chinese, had been murdered; and in 1895 a single Resident was appointed to the new State of Negri Sembilan, which incorporated Sungei Ujong.

The logical next step was the consolidation of the four protected States—Perak, Selangor, Pahang and Negri Sembilan—into a federation with a Resident-General in charge. This took place in 1896. The figleaf of advice was dropped: the Resident-General was given executive control under the Governor of the Straits Settlements who acquired the additional function of High Commissioner for the Federated Malay States. Each State retained a Resident who was responsible to the Resident-General located in Kuala Lumpur.

These actions were justified on the usual grounds that Britain had to ensure peace and order and develop communications to bring isolated districts into touch with the rest of the country. The rulers of the states were to be constitutional monarchs and the British Resident was to see to it that they behaved constitutionally. It was also desirable to arrange for representation of the interests of immigrants who otherwise would, as infidels, have had no rights in a Muslim society. The public revenues had to be devoted to public welfare not to private profit, and the administration was to be efficiently conducted by disinterested specialists instead of interested amateurs. All these were familiar arguments to support the substitution of good government for self-government, but could be strengthened by showing that the results were beneficial to the inhabitants if not so clearly to the advantage of the rulers.

In the next stage of consolidation a Federal Council was set up by an agreement in 1909. The Council was composed of the Resident-General, the four Residents, the four Sultans and four unofficial members nominated by the High Commissioner. A move to stop the centralizing trend was made by demoting the Resident-General to a mere Chief Secretary; but the process of undermining the position of the Sultans was continued by placing them on a par in the Council with four unofficial nominated members.

In 1909 also the four northern States of Kedah, Perlis, Kelantan, and Trengganu came under British protection by a treaty with Siam in which Britain surrendered her extraterritorial rights in Siam and Siam renounced her suzerainty over those four States. These States declined to be federated, and accepted not a Resident but an Adviser whose advice was somewhat less mandatory. The finishing touch was added when Johore which had come under British protection in 1885 accepted a General Adviser in 1914.

SURVIVAL OF SIAM

The Anglo-Siamese treaty of 1909 was a small part of the price which Siam had to pay for the preservation of her independence

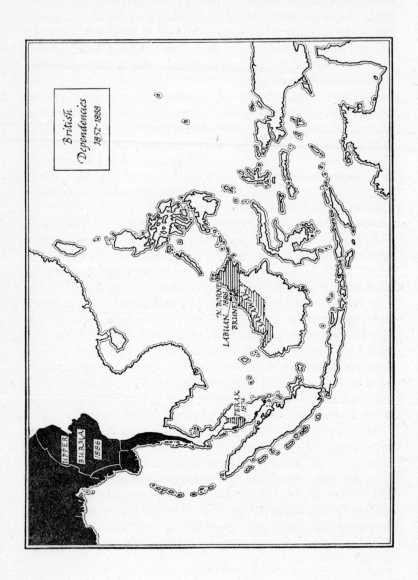

British
Dependencies
1852-1888

N. BORNEO
LABUAN 1888
1883
BRUNEI

PERAK
1874

UPPER
BURMA
1886

between the rival expansionisms of Britain and France. We have already seen the fate which befell Burma, caught between those two forces. Relations between Britain and Siam had constituted a problem ever since the acquisition of Penang, and the Burney treaty had not done much to resolve it. But after the accession of King Mongkut there was an improvement, and in 1855 a treaty of friendship and commerce was concluded which granted commercial concessions and extraterritorial rights. British economic interests expanded. The Bombay Burmah Corporation obtained the largest share in the teak industry, British firms became the most prominent in foreign trade and British capital investment exceeded that of any other country. Most of the Europeans appointed to the Government service were British.

British penetration, however, did not go unchallenged. The French were pressing upon Siam from Indo-China and approaching the Burmese frontier. They claimed the left bank of the Mekong River as part of French Indo-China, and in 1893 they sent a military expedition to enforce this claim upon Siam. French gunboats forced their way up the Menam River to Bangkok and presented an ultimatum for the whole of the left bank of the Mekong and a stiff indemnity. Only at this point did Britain intervene to seek assurances from France. The assurance was forthcoming—that France did not seek more than was in the ultimatum. Britain advised the Siamese to yield, which they did with the greatest reluctance. In consequence, Britain and France came into direct confrontation on the upper Mekong. The two countries were almost at the point of fighting, but the crisis was resolved by an agreement in 1896 by which Britain gave up her claims in return for a guarantee by France of the independence of the Menam valley. The *entente cordiale* of 1904 put an end to this rivalry between Britain and France, and each country made their own terms with Siam, subject to the limitation of maintaining Siam's independence. Thus it was that Siam surrendered to France the Cambodian provinces of Battambang and Siemreap and to Britain the suzerainty over the northern Malay States.

BORNEO

In Siam Britain's rival was France; in Borneo, surprisingly, it was the U.S.A. Throughout the nineteenth century American trade with south-east Asia had been growing, and the U.S.A. aimed at securing the same privileges as had been obtained by the European powers. In 1850 the U.S.A. signed a treaty with Brunei providing most-favoured nation treatment, but nothing came of it until 1865 when an American consul was appointed. On arrival he secured from the Sultan the cession for ten years of a large tract of Brunei —which disturbed not only Brooke in Sarawak but also the British company which was working the coal on the island of Labuan. An American Trading Company of Borneo was formed, and a settlement was planted but did not survive a year. Nevertheless, the concession was still available, and attracted the Austrian Consul-General in Hong Kong, Overbeck, who interested the Dent brothers in London. Overbeck backed by the Dent brothers, went to Borneo in 1877 with the object of acquiring the concession and selling it to whatever government might be interested, Austria being the main hope. The Sultan ceded to Overbeck and Dent some 28,000 square miles of territory in return for $15,000 a year. Overbeck then proceeded to add to this by acquiring from the Sultan of Sulu his North Borneo possessions down to the Sibuco river for a rent of $5,000 a year.

Dent and Overbeck then decided to try for a Royal Charter—a method of oversea development which had fallen into disrepute since the winding up of the East India Company in 1858. Although the Colonial Office was hostile, the Foreign Office under Sir Julian Pauncefote was well disposed. Dent made application for a Charter to Lord Salisbury, adducing arguments for securing North Borneo in order to protect the flank of the British China trade; and these weighed more with Lord Salisbury than the protests of Raja Brooke. But a general election was imminent and Gladstone was waging his Midlothian campaign, so the decision was deferred.

In 1880 Gladstone succeeded Disraeli, and Dent bought out Overbeck. The application for the Charter went forward despite the change of government, and in 1881 it was granted to the British North Borneo Company. It provided that the Company must remain British in character, must not transfer any of its grants without the permission of the British Government, must suppress slavery, must not interfere with the religious or other customs of the natives, and must follow the advice of the British Government in regard to treatment of the natives and dealings with foreign powers. The appointment of its chief representative in Borneo was to be subject always to the approval of the British Government, facilities were to be provided for the Royal Navy and a trade monopoly was prohibited.

After the publication of the Charter Gladstone wrote to Granville in puzzlement as to how it had happened, and said that he found himself in the position of shutting the stable door after the stud had been stolen; but Dilke alleged that Gladstone had seen the papers and decided in favour of the Charter against the opposition of Dilke and Chamberlain in 1880. The motive, as for the occupation of Egypt which was soon to follow, was the protection of the Eastern trade.

Subsequent events provided an interesting variation on the theme of imperial rivalry—the rivalry between the Chartered Company and Sarawak at the expense of Brunei. This developed to such an extent that in 1884 the chairman of the Company asked the British Government to set up a protectorate over Brunei. He pointed out that under the personal rule of Raja Brooke there was nothing to stop Sarawak from joining up with another country. The Government was at first reluctant, but the permanent officials were persuaded by the German acquisitions in New Guinea. The British Government decided in favour of a protectorate. Brunei resisted, but under the inroads of Sarawak was compelled to yield. In 1888 the protectorate was established over Brunei and for good measure over North Borneo and Sarawak as well. In the following year the Crown Colony of Labuan which had been going steadily downhill was handed over to the administration of the Chartered Company —but the Colonial Office took it back in 1906 and joined it to the Straits Settlements. By that time, British policy had changed and foreign penetration of North Borneo was regarded as a minor danger. It was now British policy not to accept a commitment beyond maintaining a British protectorate at minimum cost.

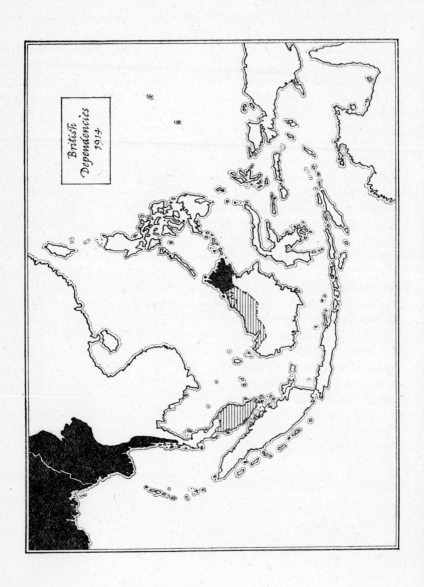

British
Dependencies
1914

BETWEEN THE WARS

3

THE CASH NEXUS

BY the time of the First World War British expansion in south-east Asia had reached its maximum extent. Burma, Malaya, Singapore, North Borneo, Brunei and Sarawak were under British control whether as colonies or protected states, and this situation remained unchanged between the wars until the Japanese onslaught destroyed in a few months a position which had taken as many centuries to build. The inter-war period therefore represents the climax of Britain's eastward expansion, and affords a useful point of comparison with the present, to measure the extent of the change.

It is usual to stress the economic motive for imperial expansion, which was certainly not absent in south-east Asia. But although the eastward quest was for trade, it was not usually the policy of either the East India Company or the Government to pursue commerce through dominion. More often than not, dominion was thrust upon Britain by pushing proconsuls like Raffles, or by the inability of the peoples of the area to keep their own house in order. However, although the flag followed trade, it is also true that trade followed the flag, and British economic relations with south-east Asia increased with the expansion of political control.

INVESTMENT

In Burma before the Second World War more than 90 per cent of all foreign investment was British or British-controlled. In Malaya the figure was over 70 per cent. In Siam the proportion was less, although of direct or *entrepreneur* investment the British and Australian portions together amounted to over 70 per cent. The bulk of the teak industry was in British hands and three out of six leading banks were British. In 1935 the country's public debt amounted to 92 million *baht* of which 87 million *baht*—about £8 million—were sterling loans: Siam was then a member of the sterling area. In Indonesia, British *entrepreneur* investment was second only to the Dutch but it amounted to not more than 14 per cent. The total in 1933–4 was £31 million of which more than

61

£26 million were invested in oil. The biggest concern was Royal Dutch Shell which was partly British-owned. In the Philippines British *entrepreneur* investment was only 9 per cent of the total and in French Indo-China it was negligible.

The amounts involved were considerable but not vast. The untold riches of the East were not in fact very difficult to tell. Adding the investment in Burma which amounted to about £50 million, in Malaya where it was rather more than £100 million, about £20 million in Siam and £10 million in the Philippines, the total came to something over £200 million. This was no mean sum but it was a very small fraction of the amount of British capital invested abroad. Overall figures can be misleading, but an assessment has been made of long-term investment in south-east Asia for 1930, excluding Burma, according to which the total amounted to £108 million. Since the total of British long-term overseas investments at that time was about £3,500 million, the amount invested in south-east Asia represented between 3 per cent and 4 per cent.

British investments in south-east Asia therefore were not a vital interest: but they had a distinctive feature of some importance—a high proportion of *entrepreneur* investments. These were "direct" or business investments made by businessmen; whereas *rentier* or portfolio investments are made by investors. The *rentier* merely puts up the money; the *entrepreneur* plays an active part. Consequently *entrepreneur* investment meant more foreign intervention in the economy of the area. It necessarily gave ris to problems concerning the relations between the foreign *entrepreneurs*, the Government and the population in the various countries: for a handful of foreigners, conspicuous in their appearance and mode of life, occupied the "commanding heights" of the economy.

In Burma three companies—the Burmah Oil Company, British Burmah Petroleum Company and Indo-Burma Petroleum Company, a subsidiary of Steel Brothers—controlled the extraction and distribution of oil, the Burmah Oil Company having by far the largest share. The other major industries—mining, lumber, rice-milling and rubber plantations—were in the hands of such companies as the Bombay Burmah Trading Corporation, which had made considerable progress since the third Anglo-Burmese war, Steel Brothers, McGregor, Foucar, Findlay, Burma Estates and the Burma Corporation. These large concerns and other smaller ones were managed by a handful of Europeans. The white population amounted to less than 10,000: that is less than one-tenth of one per cent of the total.

In Malaya more than half the rubber estates over 100 acres were British owned. Guthrie & Co., the oldest of the managing agency houses, were agents for a score of planting companies with a capital of nearly £6 million and properties comprising 32,000 acres of rubber and 10,000 acres of oil palms. The agency employed 160 Europeans in Malaya and 26,000 Asians. Not all the European employees were engaged in plantation work: about fifty of them were occupied in the agency's commercial activities. There were several other great houses of this kind—Boustead, Harrisons and Crosfield, Sime Darby & Co. to mention only the largest. In the tin industry the Chinese were dominant up to the First World War, but between the wars the position was reversed and by 1937 the European share of production was over two-thirds. A score of companies, which together accounted for one-third of Malaya's total production, were controlled and partly owned by the London Tin Corporation's subsidiary, Anglo-Oriental (Malaya) Corporation. The issued capital of the companies engaged in Malayan tin mining amounted to £18½ million, of which about 70 per cent was British. In banking the position was similar: three of the four leading banks—the Hongkong and Shanghai, the Chartered Bank and the Mercantile Bank—were British. This economic ascendancy was maintained by a British population of only about one-third of one per cent of the total.

In the Dutch East Indies with tens of millions of British capital invested in oil and estate agriculture—mainly rubber but also sugar, coffee and tea—there were fewer than 2,500 British residents.

Although the amount of investment did not bulk large in comparison with the total of British capital abroad, in relation to the number of British businessmen it was very considerable. In this sense British interests although wide in range were concentrated in the hands of relatively few people. There were also the shareholders who were concerned with the returns on investments. Any estimate of profits is bound to be somewhat arbitrary, but it was calculated that the £50 million invested in Burma produced an annual profit of £10–£12 million. In Malaya it was estimated that a profit of £10 an acre could be made on oil palms, and that this would yield on a typical estate a return of about 22 per cent on capital. These are merely specimen figures. Instances of much larger returns could be found and publicized. Whether they were excessive and amounted to "exploitation" depends upon what is regarded as reasonable profit; but it was easy to spread the view that if those industries were in the hands of the native inhabitants the profits would remain in the country. Only afterwards did it come to be realized that there might not be any profits at all.

TRADE

Investment was not the only economic interest. There remained trade.

Between 1900 and 1910 the total of British trade with the area, imports and exports, doubled—from £17 million to about £34 million. But that rate of growth was not maintained. The First World War and the inter-war depression took their toll. In 1936 the total value of British trade with the area was rather less than in 1910, although it increased by some £10 million in the following year. In relation to the total of Britain's foreign trade this was not a great amount. The order of magnitude was not more than 5 per cent. One estimate of Britain's trade with south-east Asia, excluding Burma, in 1936 arrived at a total of about £26 million which was about 2 per cent of Britain's total foreign trade. Exports were slightly larger than imports being respectively about $2\frac{1}{2}$ per cent and $1\frac{1}{2}$ per cent of the totals. Another estimate of the U.K.'s exports to the East comprising China, Japan, Malaya and the Dutch East Indies and Siam arrived at a figure roughly equal to Britain's exports to Canada alone, which was some £3 million less than her exports to the U.S.A. and about as much more than the combined value of her exports to Argentine and Brazil. So that Britain's trade to the West was considerably greater in value than her trade to the East; and in the East her trade with India was much more important than the trade with any of the countries lying beyond.

Although that trade was mostly with British territories, the reverse was not the case. Between the wars Britain took only about one-tenth of Burma's exports, to the value of about £5 million a year. Germany was almost as good a customer. Britain had a bigger share in the supply of Burma's imports: 27 per cent in 1926 and 19 per cent in 1936. But while Britain's share of Burma's imports was falling in the inter-war period, that of Japan was rising: 7 per cent in 1926, 11 per cent in 1936 .

Malaya, on the other hand, took a larger share of her imports from Britain, ranging from 13 per cent to 19 per cent between the wars, but sent a smaller share of her exports (9 per cent to 17 per cent). The value of British exports to Malaya in the 1930's ranged between £6 million and £12 million a year consisting mainly of consumer goods such as cigarettes, foodstuffs and drink, cutlery, hardware, electrical goods, cotton yarns and manufactures, vehicles and chemicals, and also tools and machinery. Britain received in exchange rubber, tin, copra and vegetable oils, foodstuffs (e.g. tinned pineapple), pepper, sago and tapioca. The most marked trend in British trade with Malaya was its decline from the dominating position which it held before the First World War. The U.S.A. became a much bigger customer than the U.K., taking the lion's share of rubber and tin. Yet, despite the decline, Britain's exports to Malaya after 1936 were greater than her exports to China.

British trade with the Dutch East Indies was comparable in quantity to her trade with Burma, ranging from £7 million to £11 million per annum in the 1930's. Britain supplied 8 per cent or 9 per cent of the Dutch East Indies imports (about £3 million a year) while Britain's imports from the Dutch East Indies ranged from £4 million to £7 million. Trade with Siam was considerably smaller. Exports to Siam in the same period—mainly cotton piece-goods, machinery, cigars, cigarettes and vehicles—were consistently about £1 million a year; imports from Siam fluctuated between £50,000 and £400,000. Trade with the Philippines was of the same order, amounting to £17 million in 1936.

Britain's interests lay not only in the goods exchanged but also in the shipping which carried them. In 1924 the value of British shipping in the region was put at £890 million. The great bulk of the trade with Malaya was carried in British ships—more than 80 per cent of imports in 1936. British ships also carried a considerable proportion of the Dutch East Indies trade—about 6 million tons out of 16 million tons a year. In 1935–36, out of some 2,000 ships entering and leaving Bangkok 440 were British. It was estimated that British cargoes worth about £1,000 million passed through the waters around Singapore every year, and on any given day British trade—ships and cargoes—afloat in the Indian area was worth £80 million, in the Australian area £50 million, in the China area £25 million.

All these were material considerations which were important to the companies and the individuals involved. Quantitatively British economic interests in south-east Asia were not such as to be vital to

E   65

her economy. Qualitatively, they had greater significance. The area was an essential source of supply of certain raw materials, particularly rubber and tin. Most of Britain's imports of those commodities came from there, as did the bulk of Britain's tea, jute, zinc, hemp and manganese and a quarter of Britain's petrol imports. By the same trade route came supplies of frozen meat, cheese and butter from Australia and New Zealand.

Political control by Britain was able to assure supplies of materials that came from British dependencies. It could also be used to protect the producers, for example by the rubber and tin restriction schemes applied to Malaya. These policies, it is true, failed to produce the desired effects: one of the main consequences, not intended, of the rubber restriction scheme was to stimulate new sources of supply outside the area. It was, however, designed for the benefit of the rubber planters, and it did restrict the expansion of the industry in Malaya, particularly of smallholdings. But this also produced an unintended result: the Government laid itself open to the charge that it was imposing restrictions on the native population for the benefit of Western investors. In the long run this did much to make Britain's position untenable: but there was the short-term economic advantage obtained by means of Britain's political control. Other examples can be given. An export duty was placed on tin ore except for ore which was to be smelted in Britain or Australia. The effect of this was virtually to confine the smelting of tin to Malaya where two British-owned companies, the Straits Trading Co. and Consolidated Tin Smelters Ltd., reaped the benefit. Another example was the imposition of quotas for textile imports after 1934, designed to protect the market for Lancashire cotton against Japanese competition. British interests also benefited from the orders for supplies which the Governments of dependent territories usually placed in the U.K.

This does not necessarily mean that Britain was "exploiting" her position. A case might be made that these measures benefited the dependent territories as well. But the point is that, between the wars, the economy of British dependencies in south-east Asia appeared to be shaped by decisions taken in Whitehall. This was a state of affairs which the people of those countries increasingly resented. The extremists condemned it as imperialist exploitation. The moderates argued that it retarded or distorted economic development. All, or nearly all, were determined to change it.

4

CULTURAL LINKS

MUCH has been written in condemnation of the distortion imposed on peoples of different culture by the introduction of English education. Even if this condemnation is valid—and it is very difficult in these matters to strike the balance of losses and gains—there is something to be said in extenuation.

First let it be clear that there was no deep-laid plot nor long-range policy. English education came to the area with the best of intentions. Usually it was introduced by missionaries or by administrators. In the one case, the object was the propagation of the Gospel, in the other, the dissemination of knowledge. Often these two motives, with typical Victorian assurance, went together.

Furthermore, although English education was at first supplied by outside initiative, in the next phase there was a growing demand for it as the key to entry into the most attractive spheres of employment. Admittedly, this demand was itself a response to the policy of the British administration which provided Government jobs for English-educated clerks and prescribed that the proceedings of the law courts should be in English. But was there any real alternative?

In theory the alien ruling power might have adopted the local language, the vernacular, as the medium of its administration; but the practical obstacles would have been insuperable. There were not enough British administrators versed in the vernacular for the purposes of direct rule; and the native languages were generally inadequate for the purposes of modern administration and education. And supposing that these two gaps could have been filled, as indeed they were to some extent over the years, there always remained the hard fact that the laws and orders governing those territories were made at Westminster, in English, and that English therefore would remain indispensable for anybody with ambitions of rising to the top. The conclusion to be drawn is that the cultural distortion complained of was not the result of this or that educational policy, but of the mere fact of British supremacy.

The complaint nevertheless is made, particularly with regard to Burma where education was widespread before the British conquest. Every village had its monastery school where boys were taught the elements of reading, writing and religion, with the result that most of the Burmese men were literate and also a fair proportion of the women who acquired the rudiments at home. This was a very different situation from that which the British found in India. Nor did it hold good of the hill tribes who were not Burmese. It was partly for this reason that the missionaries who introduced English to Burma, mostly American Baptists, tended to concentrate their attention on those who were not Burmese, especially the Karens.

British administrators also played their part. The first Governor of Burma announced that he hoped

> "to offer the people the means of acquiring a knowledge of the English language, and more useful learning than could be gained under their own system of instruction."

After the Anglo-Burmese war three Anglo-vernacular schools were opened by the Government. But the demand for English education was slight. After the second Anglo-Burmese war there were still only these three schools run by the Government. In addition various missionary societies maintained about 200 schools, but only 1,000 of the 5,000 children in them were Burmans. Then came a fresh educational impulse spreading from India. There was a proposal to develop the monastic schools and include English in the curriculum; but the monasteries did not respond with alacrity, and entered into a decline while the number of lay schools grew. The attention of the Education Department came to be concentrated on the Anglo-vernacular schools affiliated to Calcutta University, but by 1880 only nine Burmans had been able to matriculate.

Before 1900 no Burman studied at a university in Europe, and Rangoon College which was founded in 1885 as a subsidiary of Calcutta University produced only a handful of graduates a year. Up to 1918 the total was 400, and many of these were not Burmans. Some went to London, chiefly to the Inns of Court. The reasons were not far to seek. Any barrister returning with his qualifications could soon begin to earn substantial fees and become a very eligible bridegroom. He would simply mark time while waiting for the highest bidder in the marriage market, after which he could retire to a life of leisure. Or if he were more restless and energetic he would keep up his law practice or go into politics, join various societies, write for journals and generally serve as a channel for the inflow of ideas from the West.

At an early stage the system of education came under fire on the grounds that it produced Government clerks in superfluity and very little else. From the beginning of this century the policy was adopted of giving priority to primary education; but the demand was such that secondary and higher education went ahead in leaps and bounds, and in 1920 the University of Rangoon was established. It was also the Government's intention to encourage technical education rather than purely academic studies, and by 1937 there was provision for instruction in medicine, law, forestry, veterinary science, teaching, engineering, industry, commerce and art. But the total number under all these heads was less than 2,500 in a population of 16 million. Moreover, half of them were training as teachers and another quarter were in commercial schools, leaving only a quarter distributed among all the other occupations. An Agricultural College which was established in 1924 survived only six years and then closed for lack of demand. Students began to be sent to Europe for higher technical studies, but on a very small scale averaging not more than ten a year.

Small as these totals are, they are still further reduced when non-Burmese are excluded. Among university students in 1937 the number of Burmese was 32 out of 79 in law, 23 out of 147 in medicine, 55 out of 141 in education and 16 out of 54 in engineering. Yet the Burmese were 85 per cent of the population. The only schools in which they preponderated were the Reformatories (308 out of 342). This state of affairs was very much grist to the nationalist mill. Anglo-Indians who formed 0·2 per cent of the population were 8·3 per cent of the university students, and Indians who were 6·9 per cent of the population constituted 33·8 per cent of the university students.

With too many Arts graduates chasing too few jobs, there was no urgency about leaving the university. Having taken an Arts degree it became common practice to enrol for Law classes and spend a good deal of time in political agitation. The Rangoon students' union became a political force, led by students in this category. U Nu, having taken a B.A. in 1929, taught in a high school for a time and then returned to the university to study law. He was elected president of the students' union in 1935, and at the same time Aung San was elected secretary. Their associates

69

included many of the future leaders of Burma. The student strike organized by this group in 1936 takes a prominent place in any account of the nationalist movement.

In Malaya the initiative for education, as for so much else, came from Raffles, although the Malays were previously familiar with schooling in the Koran. But Raffles had a wider vision. He wrote in 1819:

> "Education must keep pace with commerce in order that its benefits may be ensured and its evils avoided; and in our connexion with these countries it should be our care that while with one hand we carry to their shores the capital of our merchants, the other should be stretched forth to offer them the means of intellectual improvement . . ."

To this end he proposed the establishment of an Institution of which the objects would be:

> "First. To educate the sons of the higher order of natives and others.
>
> Secondly. To afford the means of instruction in the native languages to such of the Company's servants and others as may desire it.
>
> Thirdly. To collect the scattered literature and traditions of the country with whatever may illustrate their laws and customs and to publish and circulate in a correct form the most important of these with such other works as may be calculated to raise the character of the Institution and to be useful or instructive to the people."

Raffles quite deliberately proposed to start at the top, on the grounds that "In every country the lights of knowledge and improvement have commenced with the highest orders of society and have been diffused from thence downwards." He provided the Institution with an endowment and with a site; but as soon as his drive was removed the project collapsed. The money was diverted to the establishment of elementary schools and the building itself was used for a girls' school. Educational development proceeded in the opposite direction to that envisaged by Raffles, from the bottom up.

It was also much narrower. Whereas Raffles had contemplated several departments and a variety of languages—Malay, Siamese, Chinese, Javanese, Burmese and Pali, as well as Arabic and English—it was English which took pride of place. English schools outstripped the vernacular schools, for the same economic motives that were operative in Burma. In the Straits Settlements there were, in 1872, three times as many children in English schools as there were in vernacular schools; but by 1900, by dint of Government encouragement of vernacular schooling for Malays, the numbers were almost on a par. In the Federated Malay States on the other hand there were four times as many children at vernacular schools as at English schools.

To encourage higher education "Queen's Scholarships" were instituted in 1886 which enabled the successful candidates to go to a British university; and Cambridge Local Examinations were introduced in 1891. But in 1900 only about 200 pupils were receiving secondary education, most of them from the Straits Settlements.

The diffusion of vernacular education was given an impetus in the twentieth century by making it compulsory for Malays in the Colony as it was in the States, and by providing vernacular schools for non-Malays. Previously this had been discouraged, on the grounds that non-Malays who received their education in their own language would tend to remain foreigners; but in 1902 a decision was taken to open Government schools for Tamils. It was an encouragement to the immigration of Indians who were wanted for work on the rubber plantations.

Government aid to Chinese vernacular schools came later, in 1923. The Chinese Revolution of 1911 and the growth of the nationalist movement gave an impetus to the spread of Chinese vernacular education, assisted by the adoption of a national language. But this did not mean any loss of interest in the acquisition of English for the material advantages that it brought, and Chinese pupils continued to occupy most of the places in the English schools as they had done from the first. Add to this the fact that higher education at Raffles College, which was opened in 1928, was entirely in English and that English was the road to advancement, and the whole emphasis of education in Malaya was clearly weighted in one direction.

This trend reflected the demand. Although the Government had encouraged Malay vernacular education from an early date, English was preferred. In 1918 the announcement was made of a new policy to meet this demand—a policy of providing free elementary education for all children in English; but numbers made this impracticable, and five years later it had to be made a long-term objective. If it had been maintained over a long period it would have had far-reaching effects on the culture of Malaya. But in the 1930's another shift of policy laid the emphasis on the development of Malay as the *lingua franca*, although strong protests were voiced from the Chinese community and even from Malays, the former because of a belief in the superiority of Chinese culture, the latter because the "bread-earning language of Malaya" was English, not Malay.

This belated switch of policy could not produce speedy results. There was little time to see its effects before the war came, and in any case English remained the language of higher education and therefore the aspiration of the ambitious. Admittedly the number receiving higher education was small. In the late 1930's Raffles College, the Medical College and the School of Agriculture between them mustered less than 500 students. To these must be added the students being educated abroad, most of them in English-speaking countries: in 1938 from the Colony there were 145—seventy-three in the U.K., forty-seven in Hongkong, one in China, ten in India, nine in the U.S.A. and five elsewhere.

In North Borneo the first attempts to introduce education were made by administrators, but the response was inadequate to sustain them. Then came the missionaries who had more success. Their schools were given Government subsidies, subject to Government inspection. In 1915 the Government established a vernacular school for the sons of native chiefs, but this too was a failure and closed down in 1930. Not until 1921 was it decided to set up Government vernacular schools on the Malayan model, and then the motives were not entirely disinterested. The Governor reporting home acknowledged the value of the educational work done by the missions, but observed that the missionary work did not appear to be altogether confined to religion and education. Difficulties had arisen over one or two cases of opposition to Government policy which were attributed to the influence of foreign missionaries. Apparently the Governor considered that Government schools would be less dangerous or at least less of a nuisance. By 1941 there were twenty-eight primary vernacular schools with some 1,500 pupils. English, which in Borneo as elsewhere was the key to economic advancement, was taught in the mission schools, of which there were in 1927 thirty-nine with about 2,000 pupils, some of them receiving secondary education. But the largest number of schools was Chinese. They had the largest enrolment but were neither subsidized nor inspected. Education in Borneo may be said to have followed the lines of Malaya, one step behind. The products were correspondingly fewer. Up to 1939 only one student passed the Oversea School Certificate.

The dissemination of English was not the only cultural impact of British control, although it was one of the most important. With English education came inevitably some English ways and customs, some of them looking very odd in their new environment. When Tunku Abdul Rahman, the Prime Minister of Malaya, was a child in Kedah the members of the Court and of the civil service wore Western dress as he did himself when he left the Palace. Frockcoats were standard wear and for very formal occasions they were made of tweed—a custom which had been borrowed from the Siamese Court. There was an English tailor in Penang who travelled twice a year to Alor Star to measure members of the royal family for new clothes. The only departure from Western style, made in deference to Muslim feeling, was the substitution of a Malay cap for the top-hat. These fashions persisted in Kedah down to 1911.

Dress is only one of the most obvious of the cultural influences. There were other outward manifestations: ways of eating, what was eaten—or drunk, social etiquette, games. It has been suggested that soccer may yet prove the most enduring of British legacies to North Borneo. Perhaps it is not altogether irrelevant that the first British territory to quit the Commonwealth was one in which cricket never caught on. Outward appearances in themselves are perhaps unimportant, but symbolize a familiarity with ways of thought imported from Britain along with English education. This influence, whether welcomed or rejected, exists and cannot be ignored.

The influence made itself felt beyond the boundaries of British rule. The proverbial schoolboy is familiar with the story of Anna and the King of Siam, at least in one of its versions. King Mongkut engaged Mrs. Leonowens as an English governess for his children in 1862. It was under her that his son Chulalongkorn, who was to become King Rama V, began his education. He was handed on to another English tutor, Robert Morant, and it is hardly a coincidence that most of the foreign advisers who were brought in under his reign were British. His Minister of Justice, who was responsible for the reorganization of the judicial system, was an Oxford graduate. In 1899 a British civil servant was loaned to the Siamese Government to advise on the reshaping of the educational system. In the 1890's also three Government schools were established for children of the upper classes, and these were directed by English teachers. Britain became the model. The school system was run on British lines and English became the second language of the educated class. Many young Siamese went to England to study, bringing back British games and dress. Rama VI, in whose reign the Chulalongkorn University was established, was educated at Christ Church and translated Shakespeare. He founded in Bangkok the Vajiravudh school, modelled on the English public school with a Siamese headmaster who had been to Oundle. He was a football enthusiast and introduced the Boy Scout movement.

The borrowing by the East from the West is only one aspect of the cultural impact. The meeting also had the effect of heightening national consciousness. In Burma, for example, the "Shoe Question" which had so often caused diplomatic friction with the Government of India in the days when Burma was an independent state remained to plague Anglo-Burmese relations. The British declined to take off their shoes when entering pagodas. At first a dispensation was given: notices at the pagodas read 'Footwearing prohibited, except to British and Europeans'. But then the younger generation of Burmese began to chafe against this privilege, and the exception was dropped. Indeed, the "Shoe Question" which was one of the causes of Burma's loss of independence was also one of the sparks which ignited the modern nationalist movement, for it was on this issue that the Young Men's Buddhist Association first began to agitate. Yet the British were slow to learn. As late as 1941 Duff Cooper relates that, when his wife was visiting Rangoon, she discovered that her British friends had never been inside the Shwe Dagon pagoda because they had to take their shoes off. She promptly removed her shoes and disappeared into the pagoda returning to a dinner-party which was subdued by her escapade. She wrote:

"We had a dreadful dinner party of ten white men and one Burman, the acting Prime Minister, complete in sarong, black-buttoned boots, native black jacket, bright pink headkerchief, and white European shirt with gold collar-stud but no collar (*de*

74

rigueur). My going into the pagoda was talked about with bated
horror. It may, apparently, lose us Burma, because, so they say,
it is a purely anti-British racket . . . My reasoning was that if they
had put on the 'no footwearing' order to keep the British out,
and the British stayed out, then the Burmese won. I'm glad I did
not know all this political significance at the pagoda gate, for I
might have then hesitated to go in. I hope I would not have
faltered as I'm sure it's all part of the Raj 'tone' here, which is
most shocking."

5

THE POLITICAL FRAMEWORK

THE development of political institutions in the countries ruled by Britain followed the path trodden by India, at different intervals. The stages of progress towards self-government, which have now become a regular pattern, were first the establishment of an Executive and a Legislative Council to assist the Governor, composed of members nominated by him; then the inclusion of elected members in the Legislative Council; then a majority of elected members in both the Legislative and Executive Councils with authority over all fields except the "reserved subjects" —defence, finance, law and order—which remained with the Governor; and finally complete self-government.

At first British Burma was governed from India. After the whole of Burma had been acquired, it became a separate province in 1897 with its own Lieutenant-Governor and a Legislative Council of nine members, all nominated. In the next stage, as part of the Morley-Minto reforms in 1909, the Legislative Council was enlarged to seventeen and included two elected members whose electorates were the Burma Chamber of Commerce and the Rangoon Traders Association, both European organizations. Although the rest of the Council was not elected, it always included a number of non-Europeans: in 1920 there were ten Burmans, two Indians and one Chinese.

Then came the momentous Montagu declaration of 1917:

". . . the policy of H.M.G., with which the Government of India are in complete accord, is that of increasing association of Indians in every branch of the administration, and the gradual development of self-governing institutions, with a view to the progressive realization of responsible government in India as an integral part of the British Empire."

What applied to India could not be withheld from Burma and the other Eastern possessions; but Burma was at first omitted from the application of the Act of 1919 which embodied the Montagu-

76

Chelmsford reforms, on the grounds that "the Burmese are as distinct from the Indians in race and language as they are from the British". The effect of this exclusion was to give a fillip to Burmese nationalism. The omission was remedied in 1923, and the system of "dyarchy" came to Burma. Under this system, the Governor had an Executive Council consisting of two members nominated by him and two ministers selected by him from the Legislative Council. The members had charge of the "reserved subjects" while the ministers looked after the rest, which included public health, education, agriculture, excise, local self-government, public works and forests. The Legislative Council was enlarged to 103 of whom 80 were elected on a franchise based on household suffrage at the age of eighteen, including women. The system was not popular: "dyarchy" became almost a term of abuse.

The system continued until 1935 when the next instalment of self-government was introduced in conjunction with the Government of India Act of that year. Under the Government of Burma Act, the Executive Council was replaced by a Council of Ministers responsible to the Legislature. The Legislature was composed of two chambers: an elected House of Representatives and a Senate half of which was elected by the other House and half nominated by the Governor. The franchise was widened at the same time to include about one-third of the adult male population and one-tenth of the female. In short, responsible government was introduced, except for the Governor's reserve powers which covered foreign relations, defence, monetary policy and the administration of the hill regions which were excluded from Burma proper. Burma had only five years' experience of the operation of this system before the Japanese occupation; but the total effect of the 1923 and 1935 reforms was not inconsiderable. Burmans became familiar with elections; a party system began to develop; some politicians acquired some experience of the problems of government; notions of law and legislation took hold. This is perhaps a too favourable estimate, coloured by later experience. At the time the results appeared in darker light. The apparent failure of political institutions on the Western model was held to be one of the "notorious evils" of Burma under British rule.

In Malaya the situation between the wars was considerably more complicated because of the co-existence of the Colony, the Federated States and the Unfederated States. This meant not only a

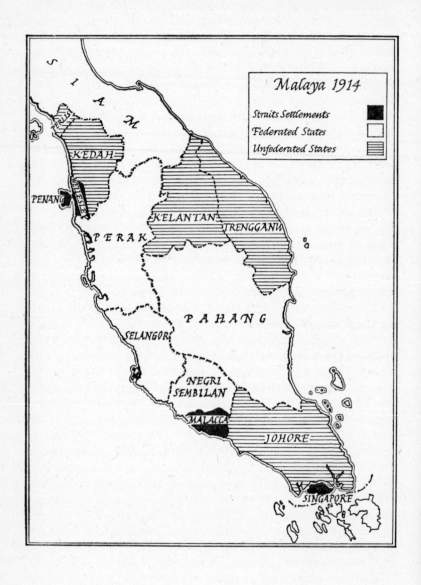

Malaya 1914

Straits Settlements

Federated States

Unfederated States

S I A M

KEDAH

PENANG

PERAK

KELANTAN

TRENGGANU

P A H A N G

SELANGOR

NEGRI
SEMBILAN

MALACCA

JOHORE

SINGAPORE

difficult attempt to marry direct and indirect rule, in course of which despite safeguards and counter-measures the Sultans steadily lost ground; it meant also that there was no plausible unit to qualify for responsible self-government, since the Straits Settlements were magnified trading posts whose population was largely immigrant and in part still migrant. Consequently the stages of development of political institutions in Malaya lagged behind those of Burma.

The Government of the Straits Settlements was of the standard colonial type. The Executive Council was entirely nominated by the Governor. The Legislative Council had after 1924 two members who were elected by the Chambers of Commerce at Singapore and Penang. The other unofficial members were nominated by the Governor with some regard for racial representation: five were Europeans, three Chinese, one Indian, one Malay and one Eurasian. As the Governor had a casting vote, there was always an official majority on the Legislative Council, but it was rarely necessary to use it. Tact oiled the wheels. Before the Second World War there was scarcely any perceptible demand for a radical change in the form of government.

The Governor of the Colony was at the same time High Commissioner for the Federated Malay States. He presided over the Federal Council which consisted of the Chief Secretary, the four Residents, the four Rulers and four unofficial members (three British and one Chinese). In 1927 the Rulers left the Federal Council and four other Malays took their place. There was nothing comparable for the Unfederated States, each of which simply had its British Adviser. A proposal was mooted in 1931 to bring the States and the Colony into a single decentralized Pan-Malayan Union. The uproar which this occasioned brought out the head of the Colonial Office who reported:

". . . from a purely economic point of view it would no doubt be advisable in a country the size of Malaya to have one Central Government administering the whole territory . . . But" [he went on] "the maintenance of the position, authority and prestige of the Malay Rulers must always be a cardinal point in British policy: and the encouragement of indirect rule will probably prove the greatest safeguard against the political submersion of the Malays which would result from the development of popular government on Western lines. For in such a government the Malays would be hopelessly outnumbered by the other races owing to the great influx of immigrants that has taken place into Malaya during the last few years."

In accordance with this policy some measures of decentralization were instituted. The Chief Secretary was demoted to Federal Secretary, and more stress was laid on the role of State Councils in legislation with a corresponding diminution in the functions of the Federal Council.

It was not to be expected that Borneo would be more advanced than Malaya. In North Borneo a Legislative Council was instituted in 1912, after an earlier advisory council had become defunct. The Legislative Council was composed of seven official and four unofficial members. The latter were supposed to represent the Chinese community, planters on the east and west coasts, and the business community. Later another Chinese was added. Thereafter the position remained undisturbed and unchallenged until the advent of the Japanese. Labuan after 1907 was part of the Straits Settlements. Brunei acquired a British Resident in 1905 following the discovery of oil. Sarawak under the Brooke dynasty possessed a Supreme Council which ceased to meet after 1927, and a Council Negri on which the native chiefs were represented and which met every two or three years to hear an address from the Rajah. There was also a Committee of Administration appointed by the Rajah, which bore some resemblance to an Executive Council; but essentially Sarawak enjoyed paternal rule. In September 1941 a new constitution was granted by the last of the Brooke Rajahs. The goal of self-government was announced and the composition of the Council Negri was widened, though not so far as to include any elected members. But the new Council only met once before Sarawak was engulfed by the Japanese onslaught.

In only one of these countries, therefore, could it be said that the foundations of self-government had been laid. The coming of the Japanese was to transform the tempo of political development, with consequences which might have been even more painful for the inhabitants had not the British left behind them the beginnings of a civil service. It may have been open to the charge of "widespread corruption", yet the fact remains that under British rule a considerable and increasing number of natives obtained some training and experience in public administration.

In Burma the proportion of British officials in the civil service declined from 41 per cent to 22 per cent between 1914 and 1942. In the top grade the drop was from 98 per cent to 69 per cent; while the proportion of Burmans rose from 1 per cent to 27 per cent. The remaining 4 per cent was Indian. The Civil Service Class I was almost exclusively British until 1923; but by 1940 out of a total of 162, two were Indians and 62 were Burmans. About a quarter of the officers in Class I of the Police Service were Asians. These two services were required to recruit half their intake in the U.K. In the other services Burmanization was still more rapid. In the judiciary the proportion of Asians to British was 187 : 13, although six out of nine High Court Judges were British.

In Malaya the process was similar but slower and complicated by racial pluralism, itself a consequence of British immigration policy. After federation the Malayan Civil Service staffed the Settlements and the Federated States and, since the Sultans would have objected to Chinese or Indian administrators, the service after 1904 was restricted to British subjects by birth or pure European descent. Alongside this service there grew up in the Federated States from 1910 a Malay Administration Service confined to Malays which by 1937 provided twenty District Officers. Later still in the 1930's a Straits Settlements Civil Service was established for which Asian or Eurasian British subjects were eligible. The tardiness of this development was due to doubts about the status of the predominantly immigrant population of the Settlements. British administrators generally regarded their primary obligations as being to the Malays; but by the 1930's they had begun to realize, somewhat belatedly, that not enough had been done to train the Malays for self-government. Policy continued very much along the lines laid down at the end of the nineteenth century which envisaged the training of Malays "with hereditary and customary claim to office" to take part in government. The assumption of the British administration was that Malay rule would be preserved through the Malay rulers assisted by a Government service manned chiefly by Malays, with perhaps, if the Malays would accept them, some reliable Chinese and Indians who were loyal to Malaya. As this service developed British administration would fade out by stages rather like a Cheshire cat. The British would first surrender their executive powers and revert to the status of advisers as in the Unfederated States; then the main body would be withdrawn leaving only departmental consultants; and finally there would be a complete transfer, and even the smile would go.

Although this process had begun, it had not been taken very far. The Unfederated States, retaining their own civil service, had done better in this respect, and in those States more of the senior posts were filled by Malays. Some of them had systems for training their prospective civil servants abroad; one of the products was the present Prime Minister of Malaya, Tunku Abdul Rahman. In Borneo the process could scarcely be said to have begun.

The political framework of government and administration in each of the British dependencies in south-east Asia before the Second World War was not uniform, but was modelled on similar lines. Each had reached a different degree of development, but all were criticized for their inadequacy. Looking back it may be thought that the strictures were too severe. Set beside the political framework bequeathed by the other imperial powers in that region the British legacy does not compare unfavourably; but this is perhaps not a very impressive criterion. More to the point was the ability of the system to recover from the shock of Japanese conquest and adapt itself to a greatly accelerated tempo of advance towards self-government. How far it was successful in this respect was to emerge in the post-war period; but before then the countries of south-east Asia had to endure the experience of Japanese rule.

6

STRATEGY AT SINGAPORE

THE passage of time since the days of Raffles had in no way diminished the importance of Singapore in British strategic thinking; rather the contrary. The reasons which led to its acquisition and retention were still operative. "It is for us," said Leopold Amery, First Lord of the Admiralty in 1923, "almost what the Panama Canal is to the United States, our gateway to the Pacific." It was appropriate that "Singapore" might be translated as "Lion Gate".

The proposal to establish a base at Singapore capable of maintaining a battle fleet was made by the Committee of Imperial Defence and approved by the Cabinet in 1921. It was said that such a base was directed against nobody in particular; it was merely a matter of increasing the efficiency and economy of the navy—part of a general insurance policy. But this made little sense unless a threat was envisaged to Britain's possessions, trade or communications in that area.

Sydney had been considered as a possible alternative for the base, but the Board of Admiralty preferred Singapore. It was the refuelling station between Ceylon and Australia, and closer to Burma, India and the Persian Gulf. It also had a strong natural position. It lent itself to defence from seaward; while the swamps and jungles of Malaya were regarded as a protection against an attack from the peninsula, especially as it was assumed that a potential enemy would have to operate over long and rudimentary lines of communication. Sea supplies could be intercepted by a strong force based at Singapore. Aircraft carriers, it was thought, would be similarly vulnerable, while attack by land-based aircraft would have to be launched at such long range as to be of little danger. Such was the strategic thinking of the early twenties. That it should have been so is not surprising: it was not easy to foresee, for example, the speed of development of aircraft and their potentialities. What is surprising is the length of time that this thinking remained unchanged.

The decision to build the Singapore base was known when the Washington Conference on naval limitation met at the end of

1921. At that conference the Anglo-Japanese Alliance was terminated, and Japan was obliged to accept the ratio of 3 : 5 in capital ships *vis-à-vis* Britain and the U.S.A. If Japan interpreted these policies as indications of a less than cordial attitude on the part of Britain it was not to be wondered at.

In fact there was no consistent British policy. The history of the Singapore base provides a notable exhibition of shilly-shallying. There was much talk about it, and a great deal of money was spent on it; but when it came to the test the base had weak foundations. The decision to proceed was taken in 1921. Three years later the first Labour Government decided to abandon the project on grounds of economy and as a contribution to disarmament. This reversal of policy was opposed by Australia and New Zealand, but approved by South Africa. The Labour Government lasted less than a year and the incoming Conservative administration ordered work on the base to proceed. But there was no urgency: it was this Government which in 1928 extended the ten-year rule—the assumption that Britain would not be involved in a major war in the next ten years—as the basis of strategic planning. The second Labour Government in 1929 again suspended work on the base, and this time its term of office lasted two years.

The next blow to the Singapore strategy was administered in 1935 by the conclusion of the Anglo-German Naval Agreement. This agreement permitted German naval building up to 35 per cent of British strength, which meant that henceforth the greater part of the British fleet would have to be kept in home waters to meet this danger. No doubt the threat would have been created in any case, but the Agreement made it certain.

The implications for Singapore were serious: for the object of the base was not to have a large British fleet permanently stationed there—Britain could not afford it—but to be able to receive the Main Fleet in case of emergency and to hold out until that force arrived. Nevertheless, such was the importance attached to Singapore that the strategy remained unchanged. In 1937 the Chiefs of Staff reported that if Britain was faced with a war against Japan, Germany and Italy, with France as her only ally, the security of the United Kingdom and of Singapore would be the keystones on which the survival of the British Commonwealth of Nations would depend. The Committee of Imperial Defence accepted their recommendation that consideration for the safeguard of British interests in the Mediterranean should not be allowed to interfere with the despatch of a fleet to the Far East. The period before the arrival of the fleet at Singapore was estimated as seventy days.

At the same time the weakness of Singapore in face of an attack from the peninsula was beginning to be recognized. In 1937 also the G.O.C. Malaya, General Dobbie, gave a warning that a landing in Malaya and an attack from the north was both feasible and likely. To meet this danger there were, apart from units of local volunteers, three British battalions in Singapore and, on the mainland, an Indian battalion at Taiping and the Malay Regiment at Port Dickson.

The basis of British strategy was laid down in a paper approved by the Committee of Imperial Defence in June 1937. That document stated that the strength of the fleet to be sent to the Far East and the time in which it would reach Singapore would be dependent upon both naval and political considerations. Nevertheless, the basis of British strategy would lie in establishing at Singapore, as soon as possible after the outbreak of war with Japan, a fleet strong enough at least to act on the defensive and to serve as a deterrent against any threats to British interests in the Far East. If Italy intervened in the war it was recognized that this would impose conflicting demands on the fleet. In that situation policy would have to be governed by the principle that no concern for British interests in the Mediterranean should be allowed to interfere with the despatch of a fleet to the Far East. This order of priorities remained unaltered and unquestioned until 1939. In March of that year the British Prime Minister, Neville Chamberlain, informed the Prime Minister of Australia that in the event of war with Germany, Italy and Japan it would still be the British Government's intention to send a fleet to Singapore. The size of the fleet would necessarily depend on the moment when Japan entered the war and what losses, if any, had been previously sustained. It would, however, be Britain's intention to achieve three main objectives:

1. The prevention of any major operation against Australia, New Zealand or India.
2. To keep open Britain's sea communications.
3. To prevent the fall of Singapore.

As the international situation in the West worsened the estimated time for the arrival of a fleet at Singapore increased. In July

1939 it was raised from seventy to ninety days: in September to 180 days. By way of compensation a brigade group was sent from India to Malaya.

There is a striking omission from all this strategic planning of any reference to Malaya except as a possible route for an enemy approach to Singapore. Yet Malacca and Penang were British territories and the Malay States, Federated and Unfederated, were under British protection. What was the meaning of "British protection" if it did not mean defence against attack? Yet we have it on the authority of Lieutenant-General Percival, G.O.C. Malaya in 1941, that the object of the defence was the protection of the Singapore naval base, and the holding of any part of Malaya or Singapore island was merely a means to that end.

In October, 1939, when the war in the West had begun, the First Lord of the Admiralty, Winston Churchill, was still giving the same high strategic priority to the defence of Singapore. In a memorandum to the Cabinet he said that the defence of Australia, and of Singapore as a stepping-stone to Australia, was next in priority to the mastering of the main enemy fleet, and that if the choice were presented of defending Australia against serious attack or sacrificing British interests in the Mediterranean, Britain's duty to Australia would take precedence. The Cabinet, however, was somewhat hesitant. Britain had by this time assumed obligations to the Turks and the French to help to neutralize Italian naval power in the Mediterranean, which made it impossible to say in advance how soon or how big a fleet could be sent to the East. But Churchill's memorandum was concerned with a serious attack as distinct from a raid, and the Cabinet agreed that if there were a major assault a fleet must and would be sent.

The British and French staffs, in preparing for the contingency of Japanese intervention, had envisaged the despatch of naval reinforcements to Singapore, recognizing it as "the key to the strategical situation in the Indian Ocean, Far East and Australasia". But there were counterbalancing considerations:

"On the other hand, if the Allies were defeated in the West, the collapse of our position in the Far East would automatically follow. Moreover, we have to consider our guarantees to the Eastern Mediterranean powers and the hope that operations against Italy will offer prospects of early results. It is thus a question of balancing risks, and the issue cannot be decided in advance; but the weakening of the British Eastern Mediterranean Fleet should not lightly be undertaken . . ."

This was a very different picture from 1937 when the priority of Singapore was unquestioned. Now an element of indecision had crept in as the result of international developments, and the importance of Singapore was weighed uncertainly against that of the Eastern Mediterranean.

As time went on the balance tilted progressively against Singapore. In May, 1940, the Chiefs of Staff reported that, in the event of Italy coming into the war, the forces that could be sent to the East would have to be judged in the light of the situation at the time. It was most improbable that any naval forces could be sent, and therefore Britain would have to rely on the U.S.A. to safeguard her interests in the Far East. But reliance on the U.S.A. at this juncture was a doubtful policy as the incident of the closing of the Burma Road was to show.

That route, from Rangoon to Chungking via northern Burma, was the main channel for the supply of American aid to China. In the summer of 1940 the Japanese were pressing for the closing of the Burma Road to cut off those supplies. The British Ambassador in Tokyo reported that the Japanese were bellicose, and the Chiefs of Staff stressed the importance of avoiding war with Japan if at all possible. France had fallen and Britain was in a critical position. The British Government, after consulting the Dominions, decided to tell the U.S. Government that unless there was a clear assurance of American support they would have no option but to concede the Japanese demand and close the Burma Road. No assurance was forthcoming from the U.S.A., so the road was closed for a provisional period of three months from July 18.

When that period expired the situation had altered in several respects. The Battle of Britain had been fought and won, and there was no longer any immediate danger of a German invasion. The garrison of Malaya had been reinforced by two British battalions from Shanghai and an infantry brigade group from India. Furthermore, there was a shift in the American attitude. The conclusion of the Tripartite Pact between Germany, Italy and Japan had provoked a strong reaction, and inquiries had been received from the U.S. Navy Department about the extent to which the Singapore base would be available to the American Fleet. This put a very different complexion on the question, and the British Government was emboldened to re-open the Burma Road on October 18, 1940.

Before that, however, there had been a great debate in the supreme military councils about the strategy of Singapore. The protagonists were the Prime Minister, Winston Churchill, on the one hand, and the three Chiefs of Staff on the other. Of course, the Prime Minister won. But the debate is interesting not only for its effect on the future of Singapore, but also as a rare instance of a conflict of views between the Prime Minister and all his senior military advisers.

The Prime Minister's view was essentially the same as the strategic concept which had hitherto prevailed: that the defence of Singapore should be based on a strong local garrison which might be relieved by a fleet, but that there could be no question of defending Malaya. Against this view the Chief of Naval Staff, Sir Dudley Pound, argued that if a force capable of dealing with the Japanese were sent to the Far East it would mean sending both the fleets which were at that juncture in the Mediterranean together with a major portion of the Home Fleet; and this could not be done. The C.I.G.S., Sir John Dill, urged the need to defend the Malay peninsula from the Japanese, particularly the air-fields from which they could attack Singapore. Sir Cyril Newall, Chief of Air Staff, also stressed the importance of the peninsula, on the grounds that if the Japanese controlled the mainland they could deny the facilities of the Singapore base to the British fleet.

These arguments failed to move the Prime Minister. In his view the threat to Singapore was less at this juncture—it was September, 1940—than the dangers on the Home Front and in the Middle East. Britain was not at war with Japan, and a conflict was not inevitable. Even if Japan did enter the war a long-range attack on Singapore would be a risky venture. It was admittedly not possible to send a British fleet at that time, but the situation might be different at the time of Japanese intervention. Air attacks alone would not endanger Singapore—witness the experience of London.

It is difficult to avoid the conclusion that the Prime Minister over-estimated the defensive capacity of Singapore. In the previous month he had told the Prime Ministers of Australia and New Zealand:

"In the first phase of an Anglo-Japanese war we should of course defend Singapore, which if attacked—which is unlikely—ought to stand a long siege . . ."

His strategic thinking was made more explicit in a memorandum to General Ismay on September 10, 1940, in which he pointed out that the prime defence of Singapore was the fleet and that its protective effect was exercised to a considerable extent whether it was on the spot or not. For example, the Middle Eastern Fleet could, if ordered, reach Singapore in a very short time and, if necessary, fight an action *en route* because it would be able to obtain fuel, ammunition and repair facilities on arrival. Even after the Japanese had landed in Malaya and begun to besiege Singapore the power of a superior fleet would not be eliminated. On the contrary, the besiegers would find themselves cut off in the swamps and the jungles. From this argument he drew the conclusion that the defence of Singapore must be based upon a strong local garrison in conjunction with sea-power. The idea of trying to defend the Malay peninsula or to hold the whole of Malaya, a country nearly as large as England, could not be entertained. He considered that the danger of a rupture with Japan was no greater, and the likelihood of an attack on Singapore, which would involve a large proportion of the Japanese fleet well outside the Yellow Sea, was remote. In fact, he said, nothing would be more foolish from their point of view. The Dutch East Indies were far more attractive to them, but the presence of the U.S. Fleet in the Pacific would always be a preoccupation to the Japanese and they were not at all likely to take a chance. They were usually very cautious, and had need to be, as they were deeply involved in China.

This assumption was essentially based on the U.S. Pacific Fleet. In November, 1940, the Prime Minister wrote to the First Lord of the Admiralty that if Japan came into the war on the side of the Axis and the U.S.A. joined Britain there would be ample naval forces available to contain Japan. The Japanese navy was not likely to venture far from its home bases so long as there was a superior battle fleet at Singapore or at Honolulu. They would never attempt a siege of Singapore with a superior and hostile American fleet in the Pacific. That fleet, in conjunction with the British navy would be able to exercise command of the seas, except within the range of Japanese-controlled territory.

Collaboration between Britain and the U.S.A. had advanced to the point of planning for the contingency of America's entry into the war. The American naval staff agreed with the British that the Western theatre would be primary and that in the Pacific a strategic defensive should be adopted; but they differed on the question of Singapore. The British regarded it as a "vital base", "the key position in the East", and therefore the correct point of concentration for the main Allied fleet. Pearl Harbour was nearly twice as far from the Japanese home waters, and as the Japanese moved south they would be nearer to Singapore and farther from Hawaii. The British therefore proposed that the U.S. Main Fleet should move to Singapore—about 5,800 miles—as soon as possible after American involvement. The Americans did not like the idea. Not merely were they reluctant to move to a foreign base and leave the American coast less protected, but they were doubtful about the defences of Singapore and the need for its retention. So far from being willing to move their main fleet, they were reluctant even to transfer a detachment.

It was against this background that the Prime Minister wrote to Roosevelt on December 8, 1940, pointing out the danger that loomed in the Far East. It seemed clear, he said, that the Japanese were thrusting southward through Indo-China to Saigon and other naval and air bases, bringing them within a comparatively short distance of Singapore and the Dutch East Indies. It was reported that they were preparing five divisions for possible use as an overseas expeditionary force, and Britain had no forces in the Far East capable of dealing with this threat. He was, however, balancing the relative dangers in the Far East and nearer home. To the Secretary of State for the Dominions he wrote on December 15, 1940, that he did not view the situation in the Far East as immediately dangerous, and did not wish to commit himself to any dispersion of forces in the Malay peninsula and at Singapore. On the contrary, he wanted to build up as large as possible a fleet, army and air force in the Middle East, and to keep this in a flexible state either for fighting in Greece or to reinforce Singapore should the Japanese intervene. Thus he still hoped to be able to hold the position both in the Middle and in the Far East, and to avoid the painful choice between the two. But the time came, in the middle of 1941, when the choice had to be made; and then the priorities were reversed.

Up to May, 1941, and even later, the basic strategy remained unaltered, although, as we have seen, certain reservations had been introduced. No less an authority than the Chief of the Imperial General Staff, Sir John Dill, was under this impression. He reminded the Prime Minister on May 6, 1941 :

"It is the U.K. therefore and not Egypt that is vital, and the defence of the U.K. must take first place. Egypt is not even second in order of priority, for it has been an accepted principle in our strategy that in the last resort the security of Singapore comes before that of Egypt."

In the following month the Planning Section of the Defence Committee took a similar view :

". . . the loss of Egypt would be a disaster of the first magnitude. No sacrifice is too great in order to avoid it, except the sacrifice of the U.K., or vital sea communications, or of Singapore."

But the Prime Minister at this juncture thought otherwise, and carried the Cabinet with him. He records in his memoirs that he retained the impression that Singapore had priority in Dill's mind over Cairo :

"For my part I did not believe that anything that might happen in Malaya could amount to a fifth part of the loss of Egypt, the Suez Canal and the Middle East. I would not tolerate the idea of abandoning the struggle for Egypt, and was resigned to pay whatever forfeits were exacted in Malaya. This view also was shared by my colleagues."

The decline of the strategic importance of Singapore in the Prime Minister's thinking touched bottom when he told General Ismay on January 20, 1942 :

"As a strategic object, I regard keeping the Burma Road open as more important than the retention of Singapore."

Such was the strategic depreciation of the Singapore base—from being second in importance only to the defence of the U.K. to a position of inferiority to the Burma Road. This is not the place to consider whether that transformation was right: that would require an examination of the grand strategy of the Second World War. But it should be recalled that, when the choice was made between the Middle and the Far East, the danger to the Middle East was actual while the threat to Singapore was only probable. Moreover, it is possible that the Prime Minister's views were affected by his being inadequately informed. He records that it was not until January 19, 1942, that he discovered that Singapore had no landward defences. Had he known this earlier, he surely would not have supposed that Singapore could stand a long siege.

WAR AND WITHDRAWAL

7

JAPAN'S NEW ORDER

IN the event, the calculations upon which the strategic planning for south-east Asia had been based were proved wrong. Churchill had been quite correct in his view that "the presence of the U.S. Fleet in the Pacific must always be a main preoccupation to Japan". What he did not and could not have been expected to foresee was that the Japanese would be able to eliminate that preoccupation by destroying the American fleet in the Pacific. By the success of the Japanese strike at Pearl Harbour on December 7, 1941, south-east Asia was laid wide open to attack. The nakedness of the region's defences was abruptly revealed.

The assumption that Singapore would be able to stand a siege until the arrival of naval reinforcements was now put to the test. At first it appeared that the situation was well in hand. Soon after the German attack on Russia in June, 1941, it was appreciated that the danger of a Japanese assault had increased. The economic pressure put on Japan by America, in response to the occupation of French Indo-China in July, made that danger still more evident. Accordingly, steps were taken to send British naval reinforcements to the East. By this time, however, the priority of that arena had declined still further. Churchill records:

"I confess that in my mind the whole Japanese menace lay in a sinister twilight, compared with our other needs. My feeling was that if Japan attacked us the United States would come in. If the United States did not come in we had no means of defending the Dutch East Indies, or indeed our own Empire in the East. If, on the other hand, Japanese aggression drew in America I would be content to have it. On this I rested. Our priorities during 1941 stood: first, the defence of the Island, including the threat of invasion and the U-boat war; secondly, the struggle in the Middle East and Mediterranean; thirdly, after June, supplies to Soviet Russia; and, last of all, resistance to a Japanese assault. It was, however, always understood that if Japan invaded Australia or New Zealand the Middle East should be sacrificed to the defence of our own kith and kin. This contingency we all regarded as remote and improbable because of the vast abundance of easier and more attractive conquests offered to Japan by Malaya, Siam, and above all the Dutch East Indies. I am sure that nothing we could have spared at this time, even at the cost of wrecking the Middle Eastern theatre or cutting off supplies to the Soviet, would have changed the march of fate in Malaya. On the other hand, the entry of the United States into the war would overwhelm all evils put together."

Nevertheless, it was decided to send a substantial naval force to the East in the hope that it would act as a deterrent. The new battleship *Prince of Wales*, the battle-cruiser *Repulse*, and the aircraft-carrier *Indomitable* were to have been the first instalment; but the *Indomitable* ran aground in the West Indies and had to be docked. The *Prince of Wales* and the *Repulse* went on without air support, and arrived at Singapore on December 2, 1941. Five days later, while one Japanese force was sinking the American fleet at Pearl Harbour, another was beginning the seaborne invasion of Malaya. The *Prince of Wales* and *Repulse* set forth to strike at the enemy, but were detected by Japanese aircraft on December 10, and sunk. Strategic assumptions were now reversed. Previously it had been a question of whether Singapore could withstand a siege until the arrival of naval reinforcements; now it was a question of how long Singapore could hold out after their destruction. Some army and air force units came through in relief convoys during January, but on a scale too small to affect the outcome. It had been assumed that Singapore would be able to withstand a siege for at least ten weeks. In the event, Singapore fell on February 15, 1942, one week after the opening of the Japanese assault on the island.

Japanese forces fanned out all over the area. Within a month from the capture of Singapore Rangoon had fallen and Java was conquered. With the surrender of Corregidor in the Philippines on May 6, 1942, almost the whole of south-east Asia lay in Japanese hands. In a scant five months all the bastions of Western power in the East had been toppled.

The inquest on that disaster has not been completed: the assessment of responsibility and apportionment of blame will long occupy future historians. One point at least cannot be contested: the Japanese victory transformed the situation in south-east Asia, while the swiftness and apparent ease with which it was achieved radically altered Asian attitudes to the West. It has often been observed that the Japanese defeat of Russia in 1905 marked the beginning of the resurgence of Asia. The year 1942 marks another turning-point. The position of the Western powers in south-east Asia rested upon prestige and protection. On the one hand, in so far as Western rule was imposed, it could be imposed with the minimal use of force because it was believed that overwhelming strength was available in reserve: in case of trouble there would be a visit by a warship showing the flag. This reputation for strength was the basis for prestige. The Japanese demolished it in a very short time. It appeared that the king had really had no clothes on after all. On the other hand, in so far as Western rule rested upon consent, it did so in return for the protection which it afforded. When it failed to protect, it ceased to have any claim to allegiance.

Field Marshal Lord Slim relates an incident which points the moral. He was sitting outside his headquarters at Sagaing when he saw a civilian motor car drive up and discharge half a dozen Burmese dressed in morning coats, striped trousers and grey topis. They were a deputation of influential Burmese officials from a number who had taken refuge in the hills opposite Mandalay. They brought with them a neatly typed resolution which had been duly proposed, seconded and passed unanimously at a public meeting. The resolution stated that the Burmese officials had received an assurance from his Excellency the Governor that there would be no military operations in those hills which were holy to the Burmese. On the basis of this assurance they had removed themselves and their families there, but now Chinese troops had entered the hills and were preparing defences. They therefore came to ask Slim to order the Chinese out and give a guarantee that the Governor's promise would be kept. Slim observes :

"I was terribly sorry for these people. They were all high officials of the Burmese Government, commissioners, secretaries, judges and the like; their world had tumbled about their ears, but they still clung to the democratic procedure of resolutions, votes and the rest that we had taught them. They brought me their pathetic little bit of paper as if it were a talisman."

Talisman is exactly right: for it is a charm which is supposed to give protection. The tragedy of the situation was not that the

Burmese clung to it, but that the British were no longer in a position to make it work.

Not only was protection not forthcoming but there was also discrimination between those who might be extricated from the Japanese onslaught. In Penang, for example, as the Japanese approached plans were made for evacuation. The traditional principle of "women and children first" underwent a modification to read "European women and children first". Only after the European population had been taken off were instructions issued that in any further evacuation there was to be no distinction of race. Not all Europeans left; some chose to stay. But such a discriminatory policy, of which this was not an isolated example, could not fail to be marked and inwardly digested by many Asians. It made talk of "partnership" sound hollow. The fact was that the British in southeast Asia were mostly transients—people who came for a time to do a job and accumulate enough to retire home, and home for them was elsewhere. On these grounds priority for the British could be explained if not justified; but it underlined the difference between the rulers and the ruled, and weakened the claim of the British to return when the Japanese left.

Britain's prestige and reputation therefore suffered a severe blow; but the Japanese failed to gain what Britain lost. The Japanese "New Order"—the Greater East Asia Co-prosperity Sphere—was no improvement on British rule; on the contrary, it was like the replacement of King Log by King Stork in the fable, although the subjects had very little option. Some groups of Asians at first welcomed the Japanese as the only means of shaking off the British yoke; but most of them were soon disillusioned. Aung San and his Burmese colleagues, having worked to bring the Japanese to Burma, then led the anti-Japanese resistance movement. This experience tended to foster self-reliance. The British had failed to defend their territories; the Japanese proved harsher taskmasters than the British. Small wonder that the Communist alternative was found attractive by some, while others adopted a policy of "ourselves alone". The contest between Communism and nationalism began during this phase.

The Japanese fostered this development in several ways. Ostensibly the Japanese objective was the establishment of a "Greater East Asia Co-prosperity Sphere" in which every country of Asia would have its place under the sun—the Rising Sun. This did not, however, exclude a measure of autonomy for some of them. As early as January, 1942, the Japanese Premier, Tojo, promised independence to the Philippines and Burma, provided that the peoples of those two countries "understood our true intentions". That understanding involved the notion of Japan as "the Light of Asia" which was assiduously propagated by the Greater East Asia Ministry but with very little success. The longer Japanese occupation continued, the less understanding there was of this viewpoint in the occupied countries. For their anti-Western propaganda, however, the Japanese found a more ready response, especially as in their denunciations of imperialism the subject peoples could, in their own minds, include the Japanese. Anti-imperialism therefore received a great impetus from the Japanese, intentionally through their propaganda and unintentionally through their presence.

Another legacy of the Japanese occupation was the boost it gave to nationalism. Anti-colonialism made its contribution to the development of national consciousness, but Japanese policy also helped. One of the tasks of the Greater East Asia Ministry was to spread the use of the Japanese language in the place of the languages of the former imperial powers. With the best will in the world this was an unmanageable task. The Japanese language required two years more study than any Western language—English, French or Dutch—and even then it was an inferior instrument for most purposes apart from Japanese poetry. Recognizing some of these limitations the Japanese policy of the next best was to encourage the use of indigenous languages, so as to break the hold of the Western languages upon the educated *élite*. This policy had much greater success than the inculcation of Japanese. It would hardly be too much to say that the present-day language of Indonesia was a direct result. Throughout the area a great fillip was given to the vernacular languages, and with it went an upsurge of national consciousness.

Another contribution of the Japanese, to be found throughout the area, was a resistance movement. The extent to which that movement proved a nuisance to the Japanese is open to question. It varied from place to place and, as in the West, the number of members of the resistance was appreciably larger after the end of the war than had appeared before. The movement probably had more effect on the peoples of the area than on the Japanese. It was in the resistance that many of the post-war leaders made their mark. In

99

the attempts at sabotage, however insignificant in themselves, a spirit of comradeship and self-confidence was born. The recognition of the resistance leaders by the British for the purposes of defeating the Japanese set the seal upon their success, and was to prove an important factor in subsequent political developments.

Anti-colonialism, nationalism, resistance — to all these the Japanese occupation contributed heavily throughout the region. In addition, the Japanese also left their mark on each country.

When the Japanese overran Burma, the former Prime Minister Ba Maw (a Cambridge graduate) was in jail for sedition. He escaped, but was found by the Japanese and appointed to head their puppet administration. Some Burmans had believed Tojo's declaration of intention to make Burma independent, but they were soon undeceived. Nationalists who had denounced the British as bloodsuckers had to find stronger terms of condemnation for the Japanese. Nevertheless, the pretence was maintained, and in January, 1943, Tojo promised Burmese independence within a year. The Japanese drafted a Declaration of Independence together with a secret agreement which retained complete control in the hands of the Japanese Commander-in-Chief. This sham independence was proclaimed on August 1, 1943, and Ba Maw became Adipadi or Head of State. At the same time Burma signed an alliance with Japan and declared war on Britain and the U.S.A. The exactions of the Japanese in manpower and materials were ruthless, and the Ba Maw régime shared the odium. But the consequences for Burma were not wholly evil.

Burma had a taste of independence, however much adulterated. The Burmese could not act independently, but at least they could talk as if they were independent. They had obtained the form; the next step was to secure the reality. Moreover, even Ba Maw's puppet administration afforded the opportunity for some Burmese to acquire knowledge and experience of the problems of government. There had been this opening under the British also, but now it was filled by a different set. Aung San who under the British had been a rebellious student was now Minister of Defence. Thakin Nu, his associate in the students' strike of 1936, was Foreign Minister. Both these men and many others who were to emerge as the leaders of post-war Burma developed the resistance movement under the cover of the Ba Maw administration. The Anti-Fascist People's Freedom League grew under their direction from 1944.

Aung San headed the Burma National Army which was very different in its composition from the pre-war army. Then the Burmese provided only a handful of officers and a small proportion of other ranks: most of the officers were British, and most of the other ranks were British or Indian or drawn from the non-Burmese races. The Burma National Army roused the patriotism of the Burmese and rallied them behind a national banner. It was these forces that Aung San led to join the Allies in March 1945. The Japanese, in building up their puppets into a sham national government, had wrought better than they knew: when the Japanese sun was setting and the Light of Asia grew dim, those who had held the shadow positions of authority were well placed to grasp the reality.

In Malaya Japanese policy was very different. There were no promises of independence. The four northern States, which had come under British protection in 1909, were handed over to Siam and the rest of the country was administered as an integral part of the Japanese Empire. As the war progressed some consultative councils were set up, and there was talk of a "New Malai"; but even near the end, when Indonesian independence was announced, Malaya was not included.

The Japanese seem to have been so concerned to exploit the economic resources of Malaya that they failed to take advantage of the political potentialities. Communal rivalries were initially in their favour. From the Chinese community, it was true, they could expect nothing but hostility, in view of the long years that they had been at war with China; and their policy of squeezing the Chinese economically by forced loans only hardened an existing attitude. Because of this Sino-Japanese hostility, the other communities which had no love for the Chinese might have looked favourably upon the Japanese conquest. At first many of the Malays were well disposed for this reason. Some of the Indians, too, were willing to seize the opportunity to strike a blow against the British, and recruits came forward for Subhas Bose's Indian National Army. But the Japanese occupation and the hardships that it brought soon dissipated this goodwill, and by the time of the surrender all communities were glad to be liberated from their liberators.

In Indonesia the pattern was similar. On their arrival the Japanese interned the Dutch administrators and prohibited the Dutch language, intending to substitute Japanese and Indonesian

101

for both. In the administration the Japanese held the higher and the Indonesians the lower posts; but the Japanese were few and the Indonesians many; the Japanese were untrained and unfamiliar with local conditions whereas the Indonesians at least knew what they had to deal with. Consequently, when the Indonesians declared their independence there was no hindrance from the Japanese, because all posts with the exception of a few at the top were in Indonesian hands. The Japanese acted merely as overseers without fully understanding what they were supervising.

The attempt to introduce the Japanese language was equally unsuccessful. Courses were provided for the *élite* of whom the Japanese thought they could make use; but it was the nationalist leaders who made use of the facilities afforded by the Japanese to develop and spread the Indonesian language. Perhaps more than any other single factor the development of Indonesian as a *lingua franca* under Japanese occupation helped to create an Indonesian national consciousness extending throughout the Dutch East Indies. The concept of Indonesia, previously an ideal for the few, became an actuality for the many.

As in Burma, the Japanese looked for leaders who would guide the inhabitants of the East Indies into the paths of collaboration, and found Sukarno to play the part of Ba Maw. There was, however, the difference that Sukarno had the reputation of a nationalist leader with a long record of resistance to the Dutch, whereas Ba Maw had a none too bright record of office-holding under the British. When independence came, therefore, Sukarno was indispensable to the nationalist movement, whereas Ba Maw was expendable.

In North Borneo and Sarawak there was no comparable response to Japanese occupation. In North Borneo a resistance movement developed under Chinese leadership, supported by some Sea Dayaks. They launched an attack on the Japanese in Jesselton in 1943. The Japanese reaction was savage, and no act of resistance on such a scale was thereafter possible. In Sarawak there was scarcely any resistance. It was not perhaps surprising, as for a century Sarawak had been cocooned in Brooke paternalism. When its rulers were overthrown there was no spirit of self-reliance to inspire and sustain a resistance movement. There was some plotting by some Chinese; but the Malays were passive. It is true that here, as in Malaya and Indonesia, the Chinese community bore the brunt of Japanese sadism and extortion; but the passivity of the Malay communities in the erstwhile British territories pointed a moral which was noted by only a few at the time but was forcibly impressed after the war ended.

Indo-China and Siam were in a different category. The former was occupied by Japan—by agreement with the Vichy Governor, Admiral Decoux. French administration continued to be recognized by the Japanese until the approach of the Allied forces led them to take over the country directly on March 9, 1945. For nearly the whole period of the war, therefore, Indo-China was under Franco-Japanese control. It was hardly surprising that the resistance movement which developed under the name of the Viet Minh was anti-French as well as anti-Japanese.

Siam was formally still more clearly linked to the Japanese, by a treaty of alliance concluded in December, 1941, and by its declaration of war upon Britain and the U.S.A. in January, 1942—a declaration which the U.S.A. chose to ignore. Siam thereby obtained better treatment at the hands of the Japanese than her neighbours in south-east Asia, and was also rewarded by the acquisition of the four Malay states ceded to British protection in 1909 together with two Shan states from Burma. But these gains were obviously dependent on the ascendancy of the Japanese, and as the fortunes of war changed so did the complexion of the Thai Government. In July, 1944, the pro-Japanese Government of Pibul Songgram was superseded by the pro-Allied Government of Khuang Aphaiwongse under the aegis of the Regent Pridi. There was no open break with Japan—that would have been too dangerous—but secret co-operation with the Allies was begun with the connivance of the Siamese Government.

By 1945 the aspect of south-east Asia had been transformed. Western prestige had been shattered by defeat. Japanese reputation had been stained by occupation. National consciousness had grown out of common suffering. It flowered into an independence movement, nurtured both by the Japanese and by resistance to them. Self-government, even though under Japanese supervision, had engendered self-confidence. If the Japanese had been able to replace the old colonial rulers, why should not indigenous Asians replace the Japanese? The drama and irony of the situation lay in the fact that while the nationalist movements in the various countries were proclaiming their independence, the forces of liberation were approaching with an agreed policy of expelling the Japanese and returning those countries to the administration of the former ruling power.

THE END OF THE NEW ORDER

The closing stages of the war in the East were marked by a divergence between Britain and America about the right strategy to pursue. There was a difference of opinion about the importance of China's contribution to the war and consequently about the purpose of the Burma campaign. The Americans wanted to come to the aid of China not only by air but also by land, and so pressed for the building of a motor road from Ledo through 500 miles of jungles and mountains into Chinese territory. In order to build this road the Americans wanted the British to re-conquer northern Burma first. The British wanted to recapture Burma, but did not want to have to do it by advancing overland across extremely difficult terrain. The south of Burma with the port of Rangoon was far more valuable in their eyes than the north; but as Churchill observed, all of it was remote from Japan and, if British forces became entangled there, they would be denied their rightful share in a Far Eastern victory. In opposition to the American view, therefore, Churchill wanted to contain the Japanese in Burma and move south-eastward so that the whole of the British-Indian front would advance across the Bay of Bengal into close contact with the enemy.

Behind this divergence about strategy lay a basic difference of approach. To the Americans the reconquest of Burma was incidental to the re-opening of land communications with China, whereas to the British the recapture of Burma was an end in itself. Moreover, the British looked from Burma towards the south—to Malaya, Singapore and eventually the Pacific—for the liberation of British territories as well as for the deployment of British forces. But the Americans did not think highly of the strategic value of a campaign which was directed away from rather than towards Japan, nor were they interested in the restoration of British rule in southeast Asia. Their aim was to keep China in the war, not to assist "British Imperialism", and the direct route to China and Japan lay northward not southward.

Parallel to this Anglo-American dispute ran a domestic British argument between Churchill and the Cabinet on the one hand and the British Chiefs of Staff on the other. This, says Churchill, was "the only considerable difference which I and the War Cabinet had with our trusted military colleagues". Whereas the Chiefs of Staff advocated sending any naval, military or air power that could be spared to act with the left flank of the American forces in south-west Pacific, based on Australia, the Prime Minister and the Cabinet held that such forces should be used for an advance eastward to the Malay peninsula and the Indies using India as their base. One of the reasons for this divergence was given by Churchill in a memorandum to the Defence Committee on February 29, 1944:

"A decision to act as a subsidiary force under the Americans in the Pacific raises difficult political questions about the future of our Malayan possessions. If the Japanese should withdraw from them or make peace as the result of the main American thrust, the United States Government would after the victory feel greatly strengthened in its view that all possessions in the East Indian Archipelago should be placed under some international body upon which the United States would exercise a decisive control. They would feel with conviction: 'We won the victory and liberated these places, and we must have the dominating say in their future and derive full profit from their produce, especially oil.'"

After consulting President Roosevelt, who expressed a preference for the retention of British naval forces in the Indian Ocean, the Prime Minister issued a ruling on March 20, 1944, that the Indian theatre and the Bay of Bengal would remain, until the summer of 1945, the centre of gravity for the British war effort against Japan. Preparations were to be made "for amphibious action across the Bay of Bengal against the Malay peninsula and the various island outposts by which it is defended, the ultimate object being the reconquest of Singapore".

He recurred to this theme in a memorandum to the Chiefs of Staff on December 12, 1944. The British share in the war against Japan, he said, might take one of two forms: either participation in American operations, or British diversionary operations designed to wear down the enemy forces and also to regain British possessions. Of the two he favoured the latter. British policy should be to give all possible naval support to the main American advance, but to keep a thrust for Rangoon as a preliminary operation to a major attack upon Singapore. "Here", he said, "is the supreme British objective in the whole Indian and Far Eastern theatres. It is the only prize that will restore British prestige in this region."

The progress of the war provided the opportunity to develop this strategy. As the American advance neared Japan it became desirable to relieve General MacArthur of his responsibilities for the south-west Pacific area. The Americans therefore proposed, in April, 1945, to detach the whole of that area, except the Philippines and Hainan, from MacArthur's command and hand it over to the British. The British reaction was favourable. Among the advantages anticipated by the Joint Planning Staff were that:

"We should establish British Commonwealth control in an area in which we have vital strategic interests from the point of view of long-term security. Our policy is that we must either conduct or at least participate in operations to capture Hong Kong. Control of the south-west Pacific area will bring us a great deal nearer this objective. It enables us to play a greater part in the liberation of occupied territories. It is desirable that the French and Dutch should deal with us rather than the Americans on questions concerning the recovery of their possessions."

Hitherto the eastern boundary of Mountbatten's command was the Malay peninsula and Sumatra. It was only on August 2, 1945, twelve days before the Japanese surrender, that Mountbatten received the directive that his command would be extended to take in Borneo, Java and Celebes, and even then the position of Indo-China was indeterminate. In these circumstances the arrangements for the liberation of those territories had to be hastily improvised.

The character of that improvisation left its mark on later developments throughout the region. There was a considerable element of chance in the evolution of south-east Asia since the war. To some writers history is a matter of general trends, the resultant of the interaction of the forces at work. On this view the countries of south-east Asia were on the road to independence and particular accidents of history could not divert that march. On the other hand, there is no denying that the march of history proceeds step by step; and the history of south-east Asia in the years after the Second World War was decisively affected by the steps taken in the weeks following the Japanese surrender. The policy applied in the area was not the policy intended by the British Government. It was modified by the Supreme Commander's assessment of the exigencies of the situation, which was itself unavoidably coloured by his outlook. It is true that the British Government accepted the modifications: but if the Japanese surrender had not happened so much sooner than anticipated, or perhaps if there had been another Supreme Commander, the emancipation of south-east Asia might have been long delayed. This thought recurs when considering the developments in each of the countries after the surrender.

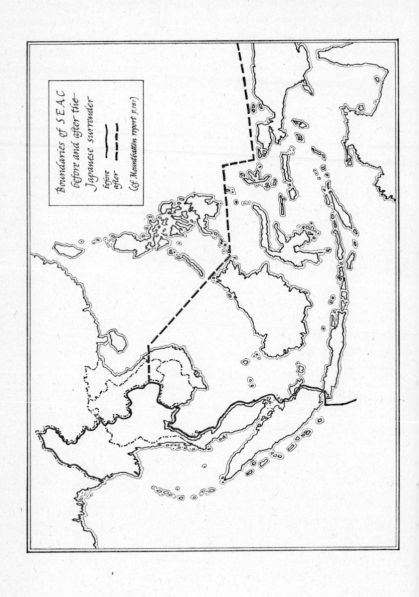

Boundaries of S E A C
before and after the
Japanese surrender

before ━━━━━━━
after ━ ━ ━ ━

(cf. Mountbatten report p.191)

8

BURMA

IT was on May 1, 1945, that an aircraft flying over Rangoon saw and reported the famous obscene message which announced the departure of the Japanese. The response was typically British: a blind eye was turned, and the bombing continued for two more days, until a Mosquito pilot decided to land and find out. This anti-climax suggests that intelligence sources within Burma were not altogether reliable. Yet contact between Force 136 (a branch of the Special Operations Executive whose task was sabotage and subversion) and the developing resistance movement had been made as early as December, 1943. Nothing came of it because the officer who was approached by the Burmese had no wireless link with the outside world. Overtures were renewed a year later; and this time the leaders of the resistance movement, which came to be known as the Anti-Fascist People's Freedom League, declared that they were planning a rising against the Japanese. The commander of Force 136 considered that this kind of activity ought to be encouraged, and proceeded to supply them with arms for the purpose. Replying to the League in September, 1944, he said, apparently on his own initiative:

". . . we take this opportunity of affording you our formal recognition as the Anti-Axis Association of Burma. We prefer to give you our wholehearted assurance of military aid only, and leave the political questions in regard to the absorption of the Anti-Japanese forces after the war to the recognized Government of Burma to whom we are referring this matter; but we should like to point out to you that it is up to the forces of the interior to show their worth, and if they fulfil the trust which we propose placing in them then the Civil Government will be unable to ignore their demands."

This policy was challenged by the Chief Civil Affairs Officer who foresaw that it would put the League in a very strong position politically, quite apart from military considerations, and he succeeded in getting the supply of arms halted for a time. But the commander of Force 136 appealed to Mountbatten, arguing that helping the Burmese resistance was a form of self-help. The problem was not confined to Burma: a similar question was likely to arise in Malaya where the resistance movement was also predominantly Left-wing. General Slim took the view that the resistance movement should be supported: if they were not with us they would be against us. Mountbatten independently arrived at the same conclusion. In his report he explains that the British had already supplied arms to some of the hill tribes for guerrilla warfare. If he were to discourage the Burmese resistance movement, he would not only lose whatever military help they might give but would also increase the operational difficulties for the forces under his command. In fact, he might find himself in the predicament of having to suppress the Burmese resistance movement by force and to divert for that purpose troops who should be fighting the Japanese. Anyway, he felt that armed action by the British to prevent the Burmese from fighting the Japanese and helping to liberate their own country could not fail to produce unfavourable reactions in Britain and America and elsewhere.

In March, 1945, when the rising against the Japanese planned by the resistance movement was imminent, the question was debated again. The military commanders advocated support of the rising on operational grounds; the Civil Affairs officers warned of the political problems which would ensue. Mountbatten again decided in favour of supporting the Burmese resistance, and so reported to the British Chiefs of Staff asking for their permission. He acknowledged that the more respectable elements of the population might be offended, but observed that those elements had remained inactive, whereas it was the politically conscious and organised element that was about to take action. He argued that although Aung San and his associates had collaborated with the Japanese they now recognized that they had been mistaken. In lending them support the British would be doing no more than had been done in Italy and other European countries where the satellites of the Axis had been accepted as co-belligerents. When the Burmese resistance forces became national heroes, as was bound to happen, the wind would have been taken out of their sails because they would be national heroes with the British rather than against them. Finally he stressed that a policy which might mean having to suppress the resistance movement by force would have a serious effect on the reorganization of the country. The Chiefs of Staff promptly referred the question to the War Cabinet, who gave their reply on March 30. Fortunately the reply was affirmative, for the rising, with British support, had already taken place. The reply is worth noting as a clear expression of the British Government's thinking about Burma at this time. It should be borne in mind that it was the declared policy of the Government to assist Burma to attain complete self-government within the British Commonwealth as soon as circumstances permitted.

The Cabinet instructions to Mountbatten warned:

"Your support of the Resistance movement, and a degree of recognition of it and its leaders thereby accorded, may have the most far-reaching political consequences; and H.M.G. attach particular importance to seeing that in the eyes of the population of Burma as a whole the movement shall be put into its right perspective. The respectable elements of the community have been inactive as yet; but the section which is now contemplating action is led by personalities who have in the past been actively hostile to us and actively pro-Japanese. Their action will not be on our behalf but by way of retaliation against the Japanese, who have let them down. Our support of this element therefore may be a source of misunderstanding and offence to elements which are less active but more dependable. It is therefore important that any support to the collaborationist leaders which we may give should not create the impression in Burma that we regard these men as the liberators of their country in any way, or that we are asking other elements to give them their allegiance. It is therefore essential that it should be made perfectly clear that these leaders must not consider their contribution of great importance, and that they must be reminded, more clearly than you suggest, that as ex-collaborators with the Japanese they have a lot of leeway to make up, in our eyes as well as in the eyes of their compatriots who have suffered at the hands of the enemy. There is a grave danger that if we do not treat them with caution, other leaders and supporters of the Resistance movement will, when normal Government returns, base upon the comparatively unimportant assistance they have given a claim for political control and possibly for immediate political concessions which H.M.G. would not consider. At all costs the building up of an

EAM-ELAS in Burma, with the unfortunate consequences that would result, must be avoided."

The role of Mountbatten was crucial. No doubt he obtained Cabinet approval, and the ultimate responsibility was theirs. But he set the course, and the decisions which he took before and during the British return to Burma determined the future political evolution of the country. The Civil Affairs staff appreciated this, and consistently opposed recognition of or assistance to the resistance movement. At the time of the fall of Rangoon they strongly urged Mountbatten to declare the A.F.P.F.L. illegal, and argued that since Aung San would now be of little value for military operations, his record demanded that he should be arrested as a war criminal. Of this suggestion Mountbatten dryly remarks:

"I had no intention, however of provoking a minor civil war in an area in which I was not only conducting a campaign but which I would be using as a base for further campaigns."

Having obtained Cabinet backing, albeit with reservations, he saw to it that his policy was understood and executed by his subordinate staff. He laid it down that no person should suffer on account of political opinions honestly held whether now or in the past, even if those opinions might have been anti-British. They would be penalized only for crimes committed or actions repugnant to humanity. He pointed out that the situation in Burma in 1942 was very complex. It was hardly surprising that the sincere nationalist elements in the country, left unarmed and unorganized at the mercy of the Japanese, should have been politically confused and should have collaborated with the Japanese, especially when promised independence. This must have appeared the only reasonable course open to them, and the British attitude should not confuse them with treacherous elements who were intriguing with the Japanese before the war, or with war criminals who helped the Japanese in perpetrating atrocities. The Japanese had betrayed the Burmese nationalists. It was now the opportunity of the British to show the politically conscious elements that they were sincere in their desire to help the Burmese to help themselves. The resistance movement had risen against the Japanese before it was clear to them that British aid would or could be forthcoming. It would be unrealistic to suppose that they would fight except in their own interests, and it was important that they should not be made to feel that their interests and British interests were mutually exclusive. Consequently British administration must contrast favourably with Japanese rule. Apart from these commonsense considerations and the natural inclination to establish good feeling between Burmans and British, the outside world would be watching the British treatment of the people of Burma during the period of military administration. He insisted, therefore, that there should be no political victimization nor any appearance of it.

In keeping with the attitude expressed in this directive Mountbatten was prepared to extend to the A.F.P.F.L. some degree of recognition. He felt that it would be unrealistic not to treat the A.F.P.F.L. as what it was: a coalition of the political parties commanding the largest following in the territory where he was conducting operations. He therefore suggested to the Governor, Sir Reginald Dorman-Smith, that Aung San might he told that the Governor would consider the inclusion of members of the A.F.P.F.L. in his Executive Council when civil government was restored; but Dorman-Smith replied that he could not contemplate giving such an undertaking.

This difference of opinion was not merely personal. It represented two distinct schools of thought about British policy on returning to Burma. There were those—often 'old Burma hands'—who felt that any recognition of the A.F.P.F.L. would prejudice future developments at the expense of the more reliable elements in Burmese politics, and to the detriment of British interests. They regarded the A.F.P.F.L. as unrepresentative and anti-British, and held that the right policy was to create the conditions in which Burmese opinion could declare itself. This school was well represented in the Civil Affairs branch and among those who had been administrators or businessmen in pre-war Burma, a coincidence which is hardly surprising since the former were in many cases recruited from the latter. The Governor himself was the most prominent subscriber to this view. On the other hand, there were those, usually concerned with military operations, who were not tied to earlier connexions and based their view on the realities of the existing situation together with a rather different vision of the future. Among these was numbered the Supreme Allied Commander, Mountbatten. It was one of the ironies of the situation, not merely in Burma but in south-east Asia generally, that the civilian element in the military administration advocated consideration for the moderates and a firm stand against the extremists whereas the military command held that the extremists could and should be won over to an attitude of responsibility and co-operation.

For a time the British Government wavered between these two views. The White Paper published on May 17, 1945, as one of the last acts of the wartime Coalition was a cautious document. It envisaged future developments in three stages: first, the return of civil government when the military situation permitted, under direct Governor's rule for a period of up to three years; then an election and the re-establishment of a Council and Legislature as under the 1935 Act. At this stage would begin the drafting of a new constitution to give Burma democratic self-government within the Commonwealth, to be instituted when the time was ripe. Dorman-Smith flew to Rangoon in an attempt to gain acceptance for this policy. He held a meeting on board H.M.S. *Cumberland* on June 20, with representatives of Burmese parties and sectional interests, including Aung San and Than Tun for the A.F.P.F.L.; but this Fabian programme had little appeal for the revolutionaries of the A.F.P.F.L. who had not planned and fought to win their independence from the Japanese in order to wait upon the inclinations of the British.

At this juncture there occurred two events which accelerated political developments in Burma. On July 26 the result of the British general election gave an unexpected sweeping victory to the Labour Party, and on August 14 Japan surrendered.

Initially there was no change of British policy. The new Secretary of State for Burma, Lord Pethick-Lawrence, telegraphed to Dorman-Smith on September 21 :

"You should certainly at this stage proceed on the assumption that H.M.G.'s policy is in line with that of the late Government's White Paper",

and warned him to resist any attempt on the part of the A.F.P.F.L. to seize power before an election. It was with these instructions that Dorman-Smith returned to Burma to resume his Governorship in mid-October. Until elections could be held he proposed to govern with the help of an Advisory Council of eleven members, four of whom he would nominate himself. The A.F.P.F.L. consented to collaborate—on condition that they would nominate the remaining seven. This demand Dorman-Smith would not accept; nor would the Labour Government to whom he referred it. At this time the Labour Government was more cautious towards the A.F.P.F.L. than was Dorman-Smith who had come to recognize the reality of the A.F.P.F.L.'s following. They were more cautious even than the Coalition. They took the view that the Governor had perhaps gone too far in the direction of appeasing the A.F.P.F.L. and might well have been stiffer. He was warned not to refer in public for the time being to Dominion status. If he had mentioned the possibility of secession from the Commonwealth, he was asked to refrain from repeating the remark. He was referred to the White Paper and recommended to avoid giving the impression that the British were buying off their enemies at the expense of their friends.

A period of deadlock ensued. The Government refused to accept the League's claim to be the only representative of the Burmese; the League took care to demonstrate its strength and influence. Tension mounted. In March, 1946, the Governor, feeling the strain and ill-advised by his subordinates, made a false move. On the basis of an accusation of murder against Aung San, made by one of his former comrades, Dorman-Smith asked the Secretary of State for permission to arrest him. Fortunately the response was negative; otherwise there was a real danger of an uprising—at any rate in the view of the C-in-C Burma. In that eventuality warning had been given by the Viceroy and C-in-C India that Indian troops should not be used to suppress it, and Mountbatten had also indicated to Dorman-Smith that there might not be any other troops available. Nevertheless, some of the Governor's advisers were pressing for the arrest of Aung San, and Dorman-Smith concluded that there was sufficient *prima facie* evidence to warrant it: the law must take its course, unless the British Government decided otherwise. At this stage the matter almost got out of control, and Burma came close to revolution: for the initial response from Whitehall was an instruction for the arrest of Aung San. The warrant had been made out and was about to be served when another telegram arrived countermanding it. This suggested a state of painful confusion and indecision in London, aggravated by the absence of the Secretary of State. Pethick-Lawrence was at this time in India on the Cabinet Mission which was endeavouring to devise a solution for that country's constitutional difficulties; but his closer geo-graphical proximity gave no perceptible assistance to the treatment of Burmese problems. During his absence the Prime Minister him-self was supervising Burmese affairs, and could hardly be expected to give them all his attention.

Such was the influence of Aung San that he had either to be in jail or in the Government. When the arrest was countermanded the Governor's next proposal was to bring him and his followers onto the Council. To this proposal a cool reply came from London. The Prime Minister said that he found it hard to follow the in-tricacies of a situation where politicians shifted their position almost every day. In particular it was undesirable to bring Aung San onto the Council while the murder charge was still outstanding. The opinion of the military was opposed to an arrest and an amnesty was being considered, but it would be better to wait until that had been settled. The proposed Council, moreover, might not turn out to be so much a united democratic front as a united anti-British front.

Not long afterwards, however, there came a change in the Labour Government's thinking about Burma. It was at length accepted that if there was to be a settlement it would have to be with Aung San. Dorman-Smith had come to realize this; now the Government reached the same conclusion, but the Prime Minister felt that the new policy needed a new man to implement it. While Dorman-Smith was on his way back to England for consultation, Attlee saw Mountbatten and asked his advice about a successor. Mountbatten recommended Major-General Rance whom he had chosen to replace his Chief Civil Affairs Officer. When Dorman-Smith landed he found that Rance was to replace him as Governor.

The new Governor arrived in Burma with the changed policy in August and was met almost immediately by a general strike, which started with the police and extended to become almost complete. The administration was paralysed. It was a very effective demon-stration of the grip of the A.F.P.F.L. The Governor negotiated on the new lines of policy, and agreement was reached at the end of September. The Governor's Council was reconstituted with Aung San as Deputy President and a majority of A.F.P.F.L. members. As the Council was given collective responsibility and the Governor proposed to exercise his powers through it, Aung San had in effect the position of Prime Minister. In that position he produced his policy of independence for Burma and now met with sympathetic response from London. Attlee announced the Government's readiness to enter into discussions towards that end, with a free choice for Burma to remain in or opt out of the Commonwealth. He said, "We do not desire to retain within the Commonwealth and Empire any unwilling peoples"—which Churchill denounced as a policy of "scuttle".

According to the Attlee-Aung San agreement of January, 1947, a Constituent Assembly was to be elected to draft the new constitution for an independent Burma. There was as yet no decision on membership of the Commonwealth, and when Aung San was questioned on that subject he replied that he personally could see advantages in remaining but the people might opt the other way. He is reported to have told Mountbatten that if it had not been for the attempt to bring a capital charge against him he would have been more inclined to press his supporters to accept Dominion status. After that their resentment was so great that it would have been useless for him to try to persuade them. This suggests that Burma's departure from the Commonwealth was caused by the ill-advised move to arrest Aung San. Perhaps this was so to the extent that it made Aung San indisposed to use his influence with his colleagues. That influence was very considerable and might have been decisive. But there is also the consideration that the A.F.P.F.L. had long been committed to the policy of quitting the Commonwealth and that, before the compromise was formulated for India, it did not appear that a republic could remain a member. The Burmese leaders assumed that India would be leaving the Commonwealth, and when it turned out otherwise it was too late to turn back, even if they had so wished.

One feature of the Attlee-Aung San Agreement was the acceptance of the aim of joining the frontier areas to the rest of Burma with the free consent of the people of those areas. This touched upon a problem which caused anxiety to the British and difficulties to the Burmese Government after the British had left. The frontier areas had not been included under the 1935 Act and the frontier peoples had no special friendship towards the Burmese. The immediate need was to associate them with the interim Government which had been formed by Aung San. This was achieved in large measure at the Panglong Conference in February, 1947, attended by Aung San in the company of the Under-Secretary of State for

the Dominions, Mr. Bottomley. Arrangements for co-operation encountered few difficulties but not all the non-Burmese peoples were
represented; in particular the Karens were absent.

The next step was to associate the frontier peoples with the working out of the new constitution for Burma. For this purpose a
Frontier Areas Committee was established under a British chairman, Mr. Rees-Williams. Reservations were encountered on the
part of a number of representatives of the frontier peoples; but the
strongest opposition came from the Karens. There was a long
history of distrust between them and the Burmese, and the antipathy had been accentuated by events in recent years. On more than
one occasion during the war the Karens had clashed with the
Burma Independence Army, and the Burmese were alleged to have
perpetrated atrocities on the Karen people. The situation was complicated by outside intervention. The Karens had been particularly
ready to accept Christianity which created a bond of sympathy
through the missionaries. They had also been especially helpful to
British guerrilla agents who had operated in the area during the
Japanese occupation. There were therefore not a few in Britain who
felt that the compulsory inclusion of the Karens in the new Burma,
which would inevitably be dominated by the Burmese majority,
would amount to a betrayal of trust. There were even those who
felt it their duty to give the Karens practical support in their
struggle for independence from the Burmese, but these activities
were discountenanced by the British Government. Burmese demands for self-determination and self-government had been
accepted; the Karen demands were not. This was another instance
of the recurrent dilemma of self-determination which, carried to its
logical extreme, would result in the creation of units too small and
too feeble to stand alone. Whether the Karens fell into this category
was a matter of opinion, but it was an opinion held both by the
Burmese and by the British Government of the day. Nevertheless,
this was not the end of the matter. The Karens National Defence
Organization took up arms against the Government of Burma.
Some of them are still fighting.

The Attlee-Aung San agreement set the course of relations
between the two countries, but Aung San did not live to see its
effects. In July, 1947, he was assassinated, together with six of his
cabinet colleagues, by hirelings of his political opponent U Saw.
U Nu took over the reins and completed the course by concluding

the treaty of October 17, 1947, in which the Government of the United Kingdom recognized the Union of Burma as a fully independent state. It only remained to proclaim that independence on January 4, 1948—at 4.20 a.m., a time which the astrologers considered auspicious. They had been correct in predicting a short span of life for Aung San; it was hoped that they would be right about this too. The last British Governor took his departure, it is said, to the tune of "Auld Lang Syne" sung by a Burmese crowd.

There are those who see in this event the consummation and justification of British rule in Burma. Perhaps, looking back, this is arguable; but the arguments are rather thin. For most of the period of British supremacy that objective if it existed was implicit only; the most explicit statement, made in 1943, when Burma was under the Japanese, declared the aim of the British Government to assist Burma to attain complete self-government within the British Commonwealth, as soon as circumstances permitted. Independence in the sense of separation was never the objective; and during the war the immediate aim was to liberate British territory and recover prestige. In the first phase after the liberation of Burma there was little disposition to concede to the demands of the Burmese nationalists. This applied to the Labour Government no less than to its predecessors. It was only when the A.F.P.F.L. demonstrated its strength and the British appreciated their own weakness that a shift of policy occurred.

The Burmese nationalist leaders for their part were also slow to take advantage of the situation. Their main effort against the British was not made until a year after the end of the war, by which time there had been a considerable reduction of British military strength in Burma and in south-east Asia generally. If the challenge had been made earlier, as it was in Malaya, it might have been less successful. Whether by luck or by judgement Aung San's timing proved correct. It may be argued that the Labour Government was committed to freeing the colonial territories, and that their attitude to Aung San initially was due not to a departure from that principle but to a mistaken estimate of the situation in Burma. However that may be, good intentions are no substitute for right policy, least of all in the eyes of an independence movement. The Labour Government cannot be absolved of all responsibility for the departure of Burma from the Commonwealth, although they deserve the credit for enough good sense to avoid the rebellion which would have occurred had the advice of some old Burma hands been followed. In sum, the Government failed to avoid a parting, but did ensure that the parting took place on amicable terms. There are many testimonials to this effect. This one from U Nu will serve for all:

> "I want to make a public acknowledgement of the great wisdom and vision of the British Labour Government. No one can deny that the British Government are in a position to drive a hard bargain with us. Yet throughout the negotiations never had I met with any instance of hard-heartedness. From beginning to end, the British Government were at pains to win our goodwill rather than our treasure."

On this basis it has been possible to build relations between Britain and independent Burma, which, if not as close as the Commonwealth ties, are cordial and fruitful.

The resumption of economic relations was a particularly delicate matter because of the extreme Left-wing attitude of the A.F.P.F.L. As it happened, during the period of military administration British and Burmese views coincided. The planning for the restoration of trade and industry in the former British territories had been based on the principle that there should be no revival of private enterprise during the period of military administration, so as to avoid undesirable distractions from the main task of defeating the enemy. There appeared to be a distinct aversion on the part of the military administration to the return of British economic interests, just as in a different field they were reluctant to sponsor the return of the missions. Quite apart from possible repercussions on the conduct of military operations there seems to have been a desire for a fresh start. British policy was not all of one piece. If economic and missionary activities were to be restricted, why was so much store set upon the liberation of Burma? The answer might be "prestige". But what was prestige for if not to re-establish as much as possible of Britain's pre-war position? There was undoubtedly a desire to make amends for the *débâcle* of 1942 and to fulfil Britain's obligations to the people of Burma. But what came after liberation? Long-term policy was marked by cross-purposes.

With the return of the civil administration there was a change of attitude. The fighting and its aftermath were over. There was no longer any obstacle to pressing ahead with economic rehabilitation, and for that purpose the return of British firms was regarded as desirable if not essential. During the war the Government of Burma, in exile at Simla, had drawn up plans for economic reconstruction by means of "projects" to be directed by the Government in conjunction with British firms which had operated in Burma before the war. These projects were not well received by the A.F.P.F.L. leaders whose Socialism and nationalism both pointed to the exclusion of foreign capitalist interests. Nevertheless four of the "projects" went ahead—for agriculture, timber, road transport and civilian supplies—operating by means of allocations from a reconstruction credit provided by Britain. The Burmah Oil Company and the Irrawaddy Flotilla Company also returned, using their own funds for reconstruction. This policy effected some restoration of the Burmese economy but also revived the old antagonism towards foreign business interests. When the A.F.P.F.L. took over the Government and the way was clear for the draft of a Constitution for independent Burma, one of the main targets was inevitably the elimination of the "projects" and the substitution of a Socialist economy run by nationals of Burma.

In the first phase of independence, accordingly, a policy of nationalization was applied, and in June, 1948, the Irrawaddy Flotilla Company and some assets of British timber firms were taken over. Compensation was offered, but not on a scale which seemed reasonable to the interests which had been expropriated, or to the British Government. The Irrawaddy Flotilla Company, for example, claimed nearly £1½ million but a Burmese commission awarded some £300,000 which the Company reluctantly agreed to accept. However, the first flush of enthusiasm for nationalization subsided rapidly as the internal difficulties of the Burmese Government mounted, and in June, 1949, a bill was passed to enable foreign capital to exploit Burmese mineral resources. A general invitation was extended by the Government to foreign enterprise to come in and develop the Burmese economy.

The policy of "joint ventures" was adopted: that is, of combined operation between the Government of Burma and foreign companies, beginning with mining and oil production. After several years of vain endeavour by the Burmah Oil Company to restore oil production and the expenditure of several million pounds, a "joint venture" was established in 1954 with the British company having a two-thirds interest and the Burmese Government one-third. By

1960 the Government had become dissatisfied with this arrangement, which gave the foreign concern a majority voice in the management of the venture, and proceeded to acquire 51 per cent of the shares so as to change that situation. In the same year the Government decided to Burmanize the import agency business. This move was delayed by representations from the British Government based on the Attlee-Nu Agreement, according to which there had to be consultation on any measure affecting British economic interests. The British protest was upheld by the Burmese Supreme Court. Nevertheless the general trend of Government policy was clear. As the Prime Minister U Nu expressed it, the aim was to divert the control of commerce and industry into the hands of nationals "to the maximum possible extent consistent with the welfare and interest of the consumers and masses".

Britain's trade with Burma was restored rapidly. In 1948 nearly half of Burma's imports came from the U.K. Then came a drop; but between 1950 and 1955 the proportion supplied by Britain remained fairly steady—about 25 per cent. In the three years 1954–7 Britain was Burma's largest supplier, having overtaken India. Then Britain was in turn overtaken by Japan in 1958. Britain's imports from Burma in the post-war period have fluctuated less—between 4 per cent and 9 per cent of Burma's exports; but most of Burma's exports go to India, Ceylon and Malaya, and Britain has not been one of Burma's biggest customers. Broadly U.K. trade with Burma has preserved its pre-war proportions; but the trend towards Japan for the supply of Burma's imports has also been resumed.

Although the friction between the Burmese Government and British concerns involved the British Government in the arguments about compensation, it did not affect Britain's general policy which was to help to maintain the stability of the Burmese Government under U Nu. During the critical phase of reconstruction and the launching of the new State, British loans to Burma amounted to about £75 million of which little more than £1 million was repaid. At the conference in January, 1950, which launched the Colombo Plan, a Commonwealth loan of £6 million was arranged for Burma of which Britain was to provide more than half. The loan was not in fact drawn upon, but the gesture of support was of considerable importance to the régime which was shaken by Communist and Karen revolt. Subsequently Burma has continued to draw upon the technical assistance available under the Plan. Between 1952, when

122

Burma joined the Colombo Plan, and 1960 the British Government spent £500,000 in supplying experts, trainees and equipment for Burma.

Most of the Burmese students who go abroad to study go to English-speaking countries. English is generally the language that they know best or the one that they wish to know better. The facilities provided and the connexions established are also contributory factors. In 1960 for example, fifty-one trainees were studying in the U.K. under the Colombo Plan. The total since 1952 amounts to 233. But the U.S.A. is proving increasingly attractive. It is easier for Asian students to obtain a place at an American university, for the simple reason that there are more places available, and there are also more scholarships to be had. It is also easier to obtain an American degree since the standards vary widely. Sometimes academic requirements are reduced for Asian students, and for some this is an added attraction.

This trend is enhanced by the decline of English within Burma. Although it remains the second language and is taught in the upper forms of the high schools, the medium of instruction at school and increasingly in the universities is Burmese. It is Government policy that teaching throughout the system should be in Burmese as soon as it is practicable. The target date for this achievement has already been passed, but the target remains. In consequence the knowledge and use of English has diminished and is likely to continue to decline: the influence of the returned students is not enough to alter the trend.

If English goes, what other connexions will remain? There is one that cannot be altered by Government policy—the admixture of British blood. Before the war there were about 25,000 Anglo-Burmese. The number was reduced by emigration, and some of them opted to be British subjects. About 10,000 took Burmese citizenship, and provided a number of senior civil and military officers as well as a member of the Government. But this has little significance. As Anglo-Burmans who chose Burmese citizenship, they might or might not retain a friendly sentiment towards Britain. In a newly established state there would be a strong temptation to be more Burmese than the Burmans. Between Britain and Burma the ties of kinship are too tenuous to be visible.

There is more substance in the legacy of laws and the constitution. The latter document was drafted largely by lawyers who had received their training at Cambridge or at the Inns of Court, and bears an English imprint. It is not merely that under Section 216 the use of English is permitted, although the official language is Burmese. That concession is not much exploited. English was sometimes used in Parliament in the early stages, but no longer. The framework remains strongly influenced by its British sources, not merely the 1935 Government of Burma Act but also the whole background of British constitutional and political thought. But erosion is in process. The Burmese political system is becoming less like the British. Democracy in Burma is to a considerable extent a British legacy, but its form has departed from the original model, and its future is uncertain.

In addition to these legacies there were also associations which independent Burma chose to assume. The Nu-Attlee Treaty was preceded, on August 29, 1947, by a defence agreement between the two countries. Britain undertook to give equipment for the Burmese armed forces and to establish a mission in Burma to train them. Britain was also to provide facilities for training at British establishments and for purchasing war materials. Burma, for her part, agreed not to accept military missions from any country outside the British Commonwealth and to give reasonable assistance to British forces bringing help to Burma or to any part of the Commonwealth. Through this agreement the new state could count on defence support from Britain and lay the basis for her own armed forces. The British mission was small in numbers, amounting to less than a hundred men, but in conjunction with the training provided at Sandhurst or Dartmouth and by attachment to various British units British influence has been considerable. In addition to this training, the predominance of British equipment gave the armed forces of independent Burma a very British aspect. They wore similar uniforms and badges—and even continued to wear British medals.

As the Burmese armed forces developed and the internal crisis which reached its peak in 1949 was mastered, the work of the British mission became less essential. At the same time its presence became a growing embarrassment, as it was difficult to reconcile with the neutralist foreign policy which the Burmese Government, following the Indian lead, espoused. Consequently, in January, 1954, the Burmese Government gave notice to terminate the defence agreement and asked for the withdrawal of the mission. The purchase of war materials from Britain and the use of British training facilities continued on a diminishing scale, but the main military link, exclusive to the Commonwealth, was severed. In military matters also, therefore, the trend is towards further separation of Burma from Britain.

By the beginning of 1954 nothing remained of the transitional arrangements which had linked Burma to Britain by inter-governmental agreements. Burma had joined the Colombo Plan, but the attraction of that was precisely that it was not simply a bilateral arrangement. Economic and cultural relations continued, but the special connexion with Britain was fading. At the same time personal relations were if anything more cordial. Now that the British no longer hold a special position they generate less hostility. Burmans can look back sentimentally to the British days, but only because they are past. Although there is widespread recognition in Burma of the value of the British legacy, it will only be admitted provided that it is not asserted. Any disposition on the part of the British to dwell on the blessings of British rule will inevitably provoke a recital of its evils. The British have left their mark on Burma, but that is not something that they can trade on. Britain's relations with the new Burma have to be established afresh on the basis of parity instead of superiority.

9
MALAYA

IN Malaya the preparations for the British return may be said to have begun before departure, inasmuch as a branch of the Special Operations Executive was set up in Singapore in May, 1941. When the Japanese attack came, this organization arranged for a number of "stay behind" groups to become the nucleus of a resistance movement. Such a movement had greater potentialities in Malaya than in Burma because of the higher proportion of Chinese among the population. Whereas the Burmese might hope for independence from the Japanese, the Chinese in Malaya after a decade of Japanese expansion in mainland China could be under no illusions. Moreover, the Malayan Communist Party, unlike the Burmese Communist Party at this time, was a reality, though not a very big one. It thrived in the resistance, and was able to control the two main organizations of the resistance movement as they developed—the Malayan People's Anti-Japanese Army and the Union which was its political counterpart.

The entry of Russia into the war and the Anglo-Soviet alliance moderated the attitude of the Malayan Communists towards the "British imperialists", and an agreement was made at the end of 1943 between the Communist-controlled resistance movement and the British command whereby the British undertook to send supplies while the Communists undertook to harass the Japanese and co-operate with the Allies in the liberation of Malaya.

There was an interval of more than a year during which contact was broken. Then as the British returned to Burma contact was renewed. On May 11, 1945, Mountbatten asked the Chiefs of Staff for instructions about the resistance forces in Malaya. He reported that there were three sections. The first was the M.P.A.J.A. and M.P.A.J.U. which, although they included a Communist element, were in his opinion primarily anti-Japanese. The second was the Kuomintang section about which not much was known. Then there was the Malay section which was small and not likely to be well organized. He proposed that the help of the M.P.A.J.A.– M.P.A.J.U. and of the Malay section should be accepted for the military advantage to be gained, and that further inquiries should be made about the Kuomintang section. The danger of accepting the co-operation of the M.P.A.J.A.–M.P.A.J.U., which were predominantly Chinese, was that in consequence the Chinese might lay claim after the war to equality of status with the Malays. Mountbatten expressed the hope that this claim might be forestalled by publication of the British Government's policy for post-war Malaya which included the offer of citizenship to those Chinese who had made the country their home. British support for the resistance movement would be conditional upon their working under British direction, and steps were to be taken to disarm the guerrillas when the fighting was over. These proposals were accepted, but the post-war plans for Malaya were still provisional and could not be published. The Chiefs of Staff also wanted encouragement to be given to the Malay section of the resistance so as not to appear partial towards the Chinese. Any association with the resistance movement was to be on a strictly military basis and politics were not to be discussed.

In August when more was known about the Malayan resistance movement, Mountbatten drew up a fresh set of proposals. He recommended that he should be authorized to accept the fullest collaboration of the M.P.A.J.A.–M.P.A.J.U. and that he should try to induce the Malays to co-operate with them, but that there should be no dealings with the Kuomintang. The reasons he gave were that the M.P.A.J.A.–M.P.A.J.U. were enthusiastically pro-Malayan, whereas the Kuomintang was communally minded and favoured the strengthening of the bonds between Malayan Chinese and China. There was also great hostility between these two sections of the resistance movement, so that it would be difficult to back them both simultaneously. He was prepared to trust the Communist Party's undertaking to co-operate with the British during the period of military administration, and in practice the secret operations which provided valuable intelligence were entirely dependent upon their support. It was true that the pro-Malayan policy of the Communists also aimed at the expulsion of the British and the establishment of a Communist-controlled Republic of Malaya in which, no doubt, the Chinese would be predominate; but Mountbatten felt that the rank and file could probably be weaned from these views if they were given equality of status with the Malays which was what they wanted most. So he again pressed for the publication of the British plans for post-war Malaya, which included Malayan Union citizenship. But these proposals were submerged by the surrender of Japan and its immediate problems, and there does not appear to have been any decision upon them by the Chiefs of Staff.

Mountbatten himself had been prepared at the Potsdam Conference for the possibility of a sudden Japanese surrender. Nevertheless the necessary readjustments could not all be made. Although Singapore was quickly re-occupied, there was an interval of some weeks before the rest of the peninsula came under British control. During that period the guerrillas flourished. They succeeded in creating a widespread impression that it was they who had defeated the Japanese. The first troops to travel south from the landing beaches near Morib to Singapore found the road open thanks to the Communist guerrillas wearing their red-starred caps who provided a kind of guard of honour on the way. There was no doubt that they were in control.

The disarming and disbanding of this force was a delicate matter. The former was never accomplished: for although considerable quantities of arms were handed in—in some cases many more than had been supplied to the resistance—there were large stocks left over by the Japanese which could be drawn upon if needed. The disbandment, however, went smoothly. Parades were held, gratuities paid and medals distributed. Among those who received recognition from the British Government for services rendered was Ching Peng, "Britain's most trusted guerrilla", who was awarded the O.B.E. Ten years later he had a price of £20,000 on his head.

The M.P.A.J.A. had been formally disbanded by the end of 1945, but this did not mean that the Communist Party and its front organization were dissolved. Their political and industrial wings took shape as the Malayan Democratic Union and the General Labour Union. At the end of January, 1946, the Labour Union called a strike in Singapore with the object of obtaining the release of some of its members who had been arrested. The strike was called off after the second day, but while it lasted it was almost complete.

Another demonstration was planned for February 15. The General Labour Union asked for a public holiday to be declared on that date, ostensibly as a day of mourning to mark the surrender of

Singapore to the Japanese, in fact as a day of celebration. Mount-batten was reluctantly persuaded by his advisers that this challenge had to be taken up, and that the only way to meet it was to strike at the Communist leaders. He refused to consent to preventive arrest, but reluctantly agreed to expulsion of those leaders who, being alien Chinese, were liable to banishment under a pre-war ordinance. The Communists made their request for a holiday and for permission to hold processions and a rally, which was refused. Rallies were held nevertheless and produced the expected disturbances, but the authorities were forewarned and strong action was taken against the demonstrators. Two were killed when the police opened fire in Singapore. Several ringleaders were arrested and some of them were expelled. The effect was salutary—the first Communist challenge in Malaya was repulsed.

This success was due to a variety of factors, one of which was faulty Communist tactics. They made their moves so rapidly and openly that there was hardly room for doubt about their nature. Moreover, at that time British military administration was still in charge and had enough troops at its disposal to meet the threat. This was in contrast to the situation which developed later in Burma. There was another point of contrast: whereas in Burma the nationalist movement could claim to speak for the great majority of the population, in Malaya the Communist-led predominantly Chinese movement could not claim to speak for more than half the population, if that, many of whom were of alien origin. Consequently the administration could count on the support, or at least acquiesence, of the majority of the people in dealing with the challenge from the minority.

British plans for the future of Malaya involved a new departure and a measure of rationalization. Instead of the Straits Settlements and the Federated and Unfederated States there was to be a Malayan Union (excluding Singapore), admitting to citizenship persons who had been born in Malaya or had lived there for ten out of the past fifteen years. It was a well-meaning attempt to recognize that many Chinese by their conduct under the Japanese had earned a stake in the country, and to foster the growth of a multi-racial Malayan nation. For this purpose, however, it was necessary to abrogate the existing agreements with the Sultans and to transfer their sovereignty so that the new Union might be instituted. Sir Harold MacMichael was selected for this job, and proved an admirable choice. He arrived in Malaya in October, 1945, and made such rapid progress that the White Paper containing the Government's proposals could be issued on January 22, 1946. In view of the indignant denunciation of these proceedings which grew to a storm soon afterwards, fanned by the efforts of distinguished former members of the Malayan Civil Service, it is well to recall that the Sultans were not so very badly treated. Several of them must have awaited the British return with some trepidation, since their conduct during the Japanese occupation could be described as collaboration. Indeed, had they been dethroned it should have occasioned little surprise. But the proposals brought by MacMichael preserved their position as traditional and spiritual leaders, and also their incomes. It is small wonder that they signed with alacrity. It was only afterwards when they were borne up by a groundswell of protest that they too joined in the denunciations.

The Malayan Union proposals evoked a strong reaction on the part of the Malays. Opposition was roused by fear of a further decline in their position in relation to the Chinese. The United Malays National Organization (U.M.N.O.) was formed in March 1946 to organize political resistance. The agitation in Britain and Malaya produced the desired effect. The Labour Government had second thoughts, and decided to abandon the Malayan Union, substituting after consultation with the Sultans and with the United Malays National Organization a Federation of Malaya. In the new Federation which was inaugurated on February 1, 1948, the Sultans retained their sovereignty and admission to citizenship was more restrictive. Whether the British Government were right to change their minds is open to question. It may be argued that the constitution of the independent Malaya established a decade later was not very widely different from the Malayan Union, and that, if the British Government had insisted, the Union would have been established and more than ten painful years of Malayan history would have been short-circuited. Not a little of the Chinese support for the later Communist revolt came from the feeling that they were second-class citizens, and it was precisely by making concessions in regard to citizenship that the Communist appeal had to be met. On the other hand, it may also be argued that the solution was one which the inhabitants of Malaya had to find for themselves and not have thrust upon them from outside; and that having reached it through the trials and turmoil of civil war the relationship between the communities will be more durable, and there will be less sense of grievance against the British. The latter seems to be true; it is to be hoped that the former will be also.

Within a few months of its birth the new Federation had to meet the challenge of the Communist revolt, and a state of emergency was declared in June, 1948. This inevitably had the effect of slowing up the advance towards self-government. The Communist revolt was unsuccessful in its aim of seizing power or establishing "liberated areas", but it did succeed in engaging the attention of large quantities of troops and police, causing heavy expenditure and disrupting the economic life of the country. It was some time before the revolt began to be mastered. The lowest point was reached with the murder of the High Commissioner, Sir Henry Gurney, in October 1951. Gradually, however, the effects of the Briggs Plan for resettling the Chinese squatters, and thereby denying food and supplies to the Communists in the jungle, began to be felt. By the time that General Templer was appointed High Commissioner in January, 1952, the balance had begun to tilt against the Communists and Templer was just the man to give it an extra push.

The improvement in the situation made possible the introduction of elections to town councils from 1951 and village councils from 1952, steps which were designed to rally the population to the Government by giving them some part in the administration. But the section of the population which needed it most was the Chinese, who provided the bulk of the membership and support for the Communist Party, and they were in many cases ineligible. In 1952 the federal citizenship law was modified to enable more Chinese to qualify. It was estimated that as a result more than 70 per cent of the population would qualify for citizenship—about 2,650,000 Malays, 1,100,000 Chinese and 180,000 Indians. The law still did not put the Chinese on a par with the Malays who if born in Malaya were automatically citizens, whereas the Chinese had also to have one parent born there; but it was a considerable advance. Concessions were also made to the Chinese in Government appointments: from 1952 an intake of one non-Malay to four Malays was established for the civil service.

The growing sense of participation and the decline of the Communist threat were reflected in the rapprochement of the Malay and Chinese communities through the alliance of the U.M.N.O. with the Malayan Chinese Association, soon to be joined by the

Malayan Indian Congress, under the leadership of Tunku Abdul Rahman. Born into the royal family of Kedah as one of the Sultan's sons by his sixth wife who was Siamese, Abdul Rahman was sent first to the only English school at Alor Star and then to Penang Free School. Although his scholastic performance was undistinguished, he was awarded the first Kedah State scholarship to study in England, and went to Cambridge where he managed to obtain a degree in history. He was, however, much more interested in sport and sports cars than in academic pursuits, and when he eventually sat for his law examination he failed miserably. Returning to Kedah he joined the civil service and became a District Officer. He wedded an English girl but the marriage broke up. After the war he went to London to complete his law studies, and on his return became chairman of the Kedah branch of the United Malays National Organization. He succeeded to the leadership of the entire movement, and when the alliance with the Malayan Chinese Association was accomplished the former playboy prince was installed at its head. As usual, this new nationalist combination demanded faster progress than the imperial power considered to be wise: in this case the demand was for an elected majority on the Legislative Council and for the elections to be held in 1954. After some argument the Government conceded elections in 1955 and an elected majority; but as it was to be smaller than had been demanded, the Alliance was not deprived of all its grievances.

The result of the election vindicated the claims of the Alliance by giving it fifty-one out of the fifty-two elected seats. In a sense it was a Malay victory: most of the votes cast were Malay, as only a quarter of the Chinese entitled to the franchise had registered. Yet it said much for the cohesion of the Alliance that, although Malay voters were in the majority in all but two constituencies, all seventeen non-Malay Alliance candidates were elected. Tunku Abdul Rahman became Chief Minister, with an Alliance majority on the Executive Council. The winning slogan of the election had been *Merdeka* (Freedom), and the Tunku had promised to work for self-government within two years. Accordingly, the demand was soon made for independence by August 31, 1957, "if possible". This represented a further acceleration of the tempo, but at a conference held in London at the beginning of 1956 the Colonial Secretary conceded the demand. It meant a transition from a wholly nominated legislature to a fully self-governing member of the

Commonwealth in the short space of two years. Interim arrangements were made for Malayan Ministers to take over additional functions from the official members of the Executive Council, and a commission was appointed under Lord Reid to draft a constitution.

The Reid Commission, composed of two British members, an Australian, an Indian and a Pakistani, duly produced their draft in 1957 which after some amendments was adopted by the Legislative Council. A compromise was arranged to allow "the Queen's Chinese", that is, Chinese whose families had long been established in the Straits Settlements, to become federal citizens automatically and at the same time to retain their status as British subjects. The independence of the new Federation of Malaya was proclaimed according to schedule on August 31, 1957. Within four years the Alliance had reached its goal.

Why did the progress of Malaya towards independence go so smoothly and speedily? Undoubtedly one factor was the existence of the neighbouring precedents, which showed that it could be done without disaster and provided some experience of doing it. A way had been found of including a republic within the Commonwealth: and an elected monarchy presented no extra difficulty. Moreover, the very fact that the Indian subcontinent and Burma had achieved independence was itself an argument for an independent Malaya. There were two arguments that could be used against it: communalism and Communism. The first was disposed of by the demonstration of the solidarity and strength of the Alliance. The second cut both ways. Although the emergency at its height was an obstacle to the development of self-government, sooner or later the Communist threat demanded recourse to the force of nationalism as a counter-balance. If the insurrection could have been suppressed by military means alone this contention would have less cogency; but as active assistance was needed from the population it was also necessary to have positive support for the Government, and that meant self-government.

These were the primary factors; but there were other considerations. The willingness of the Alliance to keep Malaya in the Commonwealth made it a more attractive recipient for the transfer of power than any visible alternative. Also both the Alliance and the British Government were agreed on the exclusion of Singapore from the transaction, although for different reasons. Moreover, along with independence was negotiated a defence agreement by which Britain undertook to help Malaya in defence of its territory and in the training and development of its armed forces. For this purpose Britain was given the right to maintain units of naval, land and air forces including a Commonwealth strategic reserve in Malaya, and thirty-year leases of land required for bases. If there was the threat of an attack against Malaya or any other British territory in the East, the two Governments undertook to consult together and take such action as they considered necessary. But if the danger was to other territories Britain had to obtain the consent of the Malayan Government before committing forces from bases in Malaya. On the other hand, there is nothing to stop Britain withdrawing troops from Malaya and using them from other bases if available.

In addition to aid for external defence Britain has been contributing towards Malaya's internal security and helping to eliminate the Communists. The end of the emergency was officially announced in the middle of 1960. At that time it was estimated that there were still about 500 terrorists left on the borders of Malaya and Thailand. Since 1948, when the emergency was declared, the terrorists had suffered more than 6,000 casualties. On the other side almost 2,000 soldiers and police had been killed and more than that number of civilians had lost their lives—356 were British.

Military aid has been supplemented by economic assistance. The total of British grants to Malaya since independence, given or promised, up to 1961 amounts to £33 million, of which £13 million were for dealing with the emergency, £8 million for the development of the armed forces, £8 million in equipment and property transferred to the Malayan forces and £4 million as a development grant. The total of capital aid provided to Malaya and Singapore under the Colombo Plan by the United Kingdom up to 1960 amounted to £60 million. In addition, expenditure on technical assistance, training, experts and equipment amounted to nearly £100,000. In the year 1959–60, the U.K. made available to Malaya more than £1¼ million, and this process continues. Further commitments of over £4 million have been made. Malaya had drawn on a credit of £2¼ million for general development, £1 million for economic development and £170,000 for the building and equipment of the University of Malaya, in addition to which nearly £1½ million was still to be drawn by Malaya from a loan made by the Colonial Development Corporation. A score of students from Malaya were attending courses of training in the U.K. in a variety of subjects—administration, transport, communications, economics, science, industry, trade and agriculture.

In this respect the experience of Malaya was similar to that of Burma: both countries have received substantial quantities of economic and technical assistance from Britain and elsewhere. In other ways, however, the economic development of the two countries has been markedly different, and shows the relative advantages and disadvantages of rapid or gradual accession to independence. On the one hand, the re-establishment of British rule in Malaya meant the return of British business interests. Within ten years of the end of the war some 250 rubber companies registered in the U.K. were holding rubber estates of over a million acres. This was more than half the area of rubber plantations in the country. A substantial proportion of these were managed by the agency houses who had also re-established themselves in Malaya: the names familiar before the war, notably Guthrie, Sime Darby and Harrisons & Crosfield, were again prominent. These houses also have interests in tin-mining; but in that industry three other agencies— Anglo-Oriental, Neill & Bell and Osborne & Chappel—are responsible for almost half the total output. Sixty per cent of Malaya's tin is produced by European-owned companies. In commerce the picture is similar. Sixty per cent of Malaya's import trade is in European hands and a still larger proportion of her exports. The agency houses are prominent in this field too. Most of them are European, with a high proportion of British personnel; but a few, notably Sime Darby, have an admixture of Asians. The largest share of Malaya's imports—about one-fifth—comes from the U.K.

The resumption of British rule therefore meant the renewal of British economic predominance, furnishing a target for attack by the nationalists and the Left. On the other hand, it has also meant a faster revival and development of Malaya's economy. In Burma the position of foreign interests was reduced by Government action, and economic revival was comparatively slow. It would be wrong to regard this as the only factor; but it is significant that the Government of independent Malaya has shown no disposition to follow Burma's example. It is true that in Malaya the elimination of the

British businessman might leave the field free for the Chinese whose economic power has long been a matter of concern to the Malays; but this was not the main reason. The major consideration was that foreign investment was the best way to economic development; and the argument is substantiated by comparing the standards of living of Malaya and Burma.

Malaya is in an exceptional economic position in that she earns more dollars than she spends. Much of Malaya's tin and rubber is exported to America and the dollars obtained go into a common pool available for the sterling area. It appears therefore that Malaya contributes much more to the sterling area than she gets from it. Does this mean that she is likely to leave it? It might seem a logical step to take, but there are counterbalancing considerations. One is the sense of economic security that membership of the sterling area provides, although this is probably not very important; but it does facilitate access to short-term and long-term capital loans. Another consideration is that Malaya, because of the wide fluctuations in prices of tin and rubber, has to accept wide variations in her foreign balances which are easier to manage in the sterling system than through an independent bank. Consequently, although Malaya seems to be having the worse part of the bargain by remaining in the sterling area, it does not appear that she would do any better outside it. Malaya's attitude might change if Britain joined the European Common Market, but first reactions suggested that Malaya in that event would want to be associated on a footing like that of the former French territories.

A good deal would depend on the general effect upon the Commonwealth of Britain joining the Common Market, for the Commonwealth and sterling are not unconnected. Admittedly the two organizations are not identical in membership, but most countries of the Commonwealth are members of the sterling area and *vice versa*. Attitudes to the sterling area therefore tend also to reflect attitudes to the Commonwealth and, at this stage, Malaya derives advantages from Commonwealth membership. At a mundane level there is the mere provision of overseas services. Full-scale diplomatic representation can be a heavy economic burden to a small, newly independent country. Malaya is able to concentrate her resources on a few key appointments and for the rest to accept the services of the Commonwealth High Commissions and the British Embassies and Legations abroad. This is no small item.

Malaya has the benefit of the activities of a comprehensive diplo-matic service without incurring the cost.

In addition to these services there is the feeling of belonging to a wider fraternity. The two main links of the new Commonwealth have been the similarity of institutions and a single language of communication—English. Malaya shares both of these. Parlia-mentary democracy on the Westminster model has been trans-planted and appears to have taken root. So has the English language. In the constitution there is provision for official use of English for a minimum of ten years, but the demand is increasing rather than diminishing. In 1960 there were 300,000 enrolments in English-medium schools as compared with 460,000 in Malay-medium, 420,000 in Chinese-medium, and 50,000 in Indian-medium schools. The branch of the University of Malaya at Kuala Lumpur has now been organized as a separate Division, and the teaching is in English. The Malayan Government runs two teacher-training colleges[1] in the U.K. with an enrolment of 450. In addi-tion, to take 1955 as a sample year, there were 685 Malayan students receiving higher education in the U.K. The awards of Queen's Fellowships and Scholarships continue, and are highly prized.*

On the basis of institutions and language Malaya feels very much at home in the Commonwealth. More than that, she has made a distinctive contribution. The Malayan Prime Minister was one of those who evoked and insisted upon the principle of non-discrimination between races at the conference in 1961, which re-sulted in South Africa's departure from the Commonwealth. That the Commonwealth has explicitly adopted this principle is in no small measure due to Malaya.

These links—economic, cultural and Commonwealth—as well as mutual defence arrangements, bind Malaya and Britain together. But there are factors which tend to separate them. Malaya has not joined S.E.A.T.O., and shows no sign of doing so. The Malayan Government is resolutely anti-Communist, but prefers not to under-take this commitment. It is an attitude which has its advantages: in the Laos crisis of 1961, for example, Malaya was able, from her position of semi-detachment, to play a useful mediatory role.

Malaya also has the ambition of leading the countries of south-

* One for students at Brinsford Lodge, Wolverhampton, and one for qualified teachers at Kirkby.

east Asia towards regional co-operation which is not afforded by the limited membership of S.E.A.T.O. With that object the Prime Minister put forward a proposal early in 1959 for a South-East Asian Economic and Friendship Treaty but met with a lukewarm response. In July, 1960, it materialized in a looser form as the Association of South-East Asian States (A.S.A.S.) modelled on the Nordic Council. But the response was still limited to Thailand and the Philippines who, being members of S.E.A.T.O., tend to deter other countries in the area from joining.

Tunku Abdul Rahman is not a man to be easily discouraged. His aim is the closer association of the countries of south-east Asia. In May, 1961, while maintaining his support for A.S.A.S.—later renamed A.S.A. (Association of South-East Asia)—he added the suggestion that, sooner or later, there would have to be an understanding between Malaya and the territories of Singapore, North Borneo, Brunei and Sarawak.[1] This suggestion coincided with the policy which the British Government had been trying, without much success, to get accepted in the Borneo territories. It stood a better chance coming from the Prime Minister of Malaya. But the first step towards such a grouping required an agreement between Malaya and Singapore.

[1] A wider association was advocated by the Pan-Malayan Islamic Party which proposed that the Phillipines and Indonesia should be invited to join in a Malaysian federation; but in May, 1962, this motion was overwhelmingly rejected in the Malayan House of Representatives.

IO

SINGAPORE

THE British regained Singapore, "the gateway of the East," on September 5, 1945. In comparison with Rangoon the city was relatively undamaged, and was quickly made a going concern. Military administration continued until April 1, 1946. On that date, with the introduction of the Malayan Union, Singapore was separated from the mainland. It was no longer part of the Straits Settlements, but a separate colony. The other Straits Settlements, Penang and Malacca, were incorporated in the Union. Labuan was transferred to North Borneo. Christmas Island and the Cocos Islands continued to be attached to Singapore. It was stated at the time (January, 1946) that it was "no part of the policy of H.M.G. to preclude or prejudice in any way the fusion of Singapore and the Malayan Union in a wider union at a later date should it be considered that such a course were desirable". But at that juncture it was not favoured, for two main reasons.

The first was the island's racial composition. The majority of its inhabitants had always been Chinese. In 1947 the population of the island was 930,000 of which three-quarters were Chinese. More significant than this figure was the fact that, counting the whole population of Malaya and Singapore, the Chinese amounted to 45 per cent and Malays to 43·3 per cent; whereas if Singapore were not included the proportions changed to Malays 49·5 per cent and Chinese 38·4 per cent. Simply stated, the inclusion of Singapore would upet the racial preponderance of the Malays.

The second main reason for the separation was economic. It had been Raffles's policy to make Singapore a free port, and so it had remained. Its growth and success depended upon that status. The peninsula on the other hand had very little *entrepôt* trade. It exported raw materials and imported manufactures, and drew three-fifths of its revenue from import and export duties. There was therefore a divergence of outlook. But there was also some common interest: for most of Malaya's imports and exports passed through Singapore, and this commerce tended to bulk larger in Singapore's economy as the pattern of trade altered in the region. Subsequent

139

developments have led to greater stress being placed on the need to join Singapore with the mainland; but when the Malayan Union was replaced by the Federation in 1948 the separation was maintained.

The Government which was established in 1946 was composed of the Governor assisted by an Executive and Legislative Council. The Executive Council was entirely nominated by the Governor, but the composition of the Legislative Council represented an advance on the pre-war constitution in that it had a majority of unofficial members and most of them were elected. Three were chosen by the Chambers of Commerce—European, Chinese and Indian; the other six were directly elected on a very liberal franchise. The vote was given to all British subjects, men and women, over 21. The response, however, was slight. For the first election held in March, 1948, the potential electorate was estimated at about 200,000; but only a tenth of that number registered, and nearly half of them were Indians. The Chinese were apparently not interested. Elections to the Legislative Council were held again in 1951 and on this occasion the registration was doubled, although it was still only about one-fifth of the potential electorate. Again the Indians showed more interest than the Chinese.

In 1954 the Rendel Commission reported in favour of establishing a Legislative Assembly and a Council of Ministers. The former was to be composed of thirty-two members, twenty-five of them elected directly, and the remainder nominated by the Governor. The Council of Ministers was to be composed of nine members apart from the Governor, three of them *ex officio* and the rest chosen by the majority in the Assembly. It was to be a system of dyarchy. The *ex officio* Ministers were responsible to the Governor for finance, external affairs, defence and internal security, while other departments would be in charge of elected Ministers responsible to the Assembly. The leader of the largest party in the Assembly would have the title of Chief Minister and perform the functions of a Prime Minister in the area outside the reserved subjects. The Governor retained emergency powers, but they were not intended for use if it could be avoided. For the Assembly elections automatic registration of voters was recommended. The size of the electorate was estimated as 282,000 out of a population of 1,120,000, and more than half the electorate was Chinese. But only 83,000 voters were literate in English, and most of those were not Chinese, yet the official language of the Assembly was English.

The first Government established under the new constitution, headed by David Marshall, inevitably asked for more. Its policy was self-government for Singapore, but its leader was unable to obtain the consent of the British Government or to retain the confidence of his followers. In 1956 Marshall was succeeded by his colleague Lim Yew Hock who led an all-party delegation to London in the spring of 1957. The British Government agreed to the constitution of a State of Singapore with full internal self-government and a Singapore citizenship. The Governor was to be replaced by a Head of State (Yang di-Pertuan Negara) with a Council of Ministers led by a Prime Minister and an elected legislative assembly of fifty-one members. For a transitional period the post of Head of State and U.K. Commissioner were combined, but they were later to be separated and the U.K. Commissioner would then be responsible only for defence and external affairs. Internal security was the responsibility of the Singapore Government; but since it had a bearing on external defence all these matters were to come within the purview of an Internal Security Council composed of the Prime Minister and two other Ministers, the U.K. Commissioner and two other British representatives, and one Minister from the Federation of Malaya who would in effect have the casting vote. The Federation Government in agreeing to this proposal accepted a link between Singapore and the Federation, and so obtained access to all information relating to internal security in Singapore.

By legislation passed in September, 1957, citizenship became the right of all those who were born in Singapore, and was open to others by registration after a specified period of residence providing that they took an oath of allegiance. As a result of this liberalization the registered electorate of Singapore which was 22,000 in 1948 and 300,000 in 1955, leaped to 600,000 in 1958.

In May, 1958, there was another all-party mission which settled details of the new constitution. The British Government insisted on the stipulation that those who were under detention should not be allowed to stand for election to the first Assembly. This was formally resisted, although there is reason to believe that several of the delegation were privately pleased to have this danger conveniently removed, with the onus resting upon the British Government.

When the new constitution had been through the necessary processes at Westminster, Singapore went to the polls. The result of the election held on May 30, 1959, was an overwhelming victory for the People's Action Party which won forty-three out of fifty-one seats. The State of Singapore was formally inaugurated on June 3 and the former Governor became Head of State and U.K. Commissioner. He called upon Lee Kuan Yew, the leader of the P.A.P., to form a Government. The new Prime Minister was third generation Straits Chinese, born of a prosperous merchant family and was able to go to Cambridge to take a degree in Law. Of the eight other members of the Government two were products of London University and another of Oxford. Consequently a large part of the new Government, comprising the most important members of it, was educated in Britain. This did not necessarily mean that they retained any particular affection for that country. In one or two cases their experiences of the U.K. seemed to have left them embittered and hostile. Yet the educational background which they had acquired could not be shaken off as the political association could be. Sometimes it had its uses. When in June, 1959, the Prime Minister of Singapore met the Prime Minister of the Federation (at that time Dato Abdul Razak) he observed that they had been friends for many years, both when they were students at Raffles College and later when Razak was in London and Lee Kuan Yew at Cambridge.

As its representative on the Security Council the Federation of Malaya nominated the Minister for External Affairs. In December another Malay, brother of the Minister of Agriculture in the Federation, took office as Head of State and so completed the constitutional arrangements for the new State of Singapore. These dispositions were recognized as temporary and transitional. It was not supposed that Singapore would remain indefinitely in this half-way house to complete self-government. But the next stage of development was not predetermined. The move could be made in more than one direction; and the P.A.P. as the ruling party had definite ideas about the line of advance.

The P.A.P. began by being determinedly "not anti-Communist". There had been a Communist section of the party, and one of the first steps of the new Government was to secure the release of its members who had been detained. The Government itself represented a combination of moderate and extremist factions, and an internal struggle ensued culminating, in the middle of 1960, with the expulsion of the leader of the Left-wing faction from the Government and from the Party. This action indicated that the moderates were in control, at least for the time being.

One of the chief reasons for this development was the desire of the P.A.P. to achieve the association of Singapore with the Federation. The motives for this were mixed. It was recognized that full self-government for Singapore alone would be much more difficult to obtain, if possible at all, and that the process might be quickened by joining with independent Malaya. There was also the consideration that Singapore had become increasingly dependent upon trade with the Federation and that its economic prospects point in that direction. Accordingly the P.A.P. Government of Singapore has been concerned not to alienate the Government of the Federation, and to provide reassurance that it is able and willing to control Communism. It has also accepted the principle that the official language of Singapore shall be Malay, in spite of the fact that the great majority of the population is Chinese.

The 1957 population census gave the following results:

Chinese	1,090,595
Malaysians	197,060
Indians and Pakistanis ...	124,084
Europeans	10,826
Eurasian	11,382
Others	11,982
	—1,445,929

Of this total more than half were under 25. Most of them (64 per cent) were born in Singapore itself, and another 8·6 in the Federation. Two hundred thousand were able to read and write English. The literacy in Chinese was only 50,000 more. The other main languages are Malay and Tamil. This mixture of races presents a major educational problem.

The policy adopted in 1957 was to recognize all four languages as media of education. There were to be Malay, Chinese, English and Tamil schools, with English compulsory in the non-English schools as a second language and one of the others compulsory in the English schools. In 1958 the number of pupils in English-medium schools was about half the total. Secondary education was provided only in English- and Chinese-medium schools. In the University of Malaya, established in 1949, where the medium of instruction is

143

English, there were in 1958 1,600 students of whom 1,000 were Chinese. The Nanyang University, founded in protest in 1956, has Chinese medium of instruction and its enrolment is comparable if not its standards.

Under the P.A.P. Government the language policy was changed and Malay was to be taught in all schools: primary schools were to be bilingual in Malay and one other language. But in 1959 a census showed that, of the 88,000 people who could read and write Malay, only 13,000 were non-Malays. Singapore has a long way to go along the road of Malayanization before it is likely to be acceptable as a partner to the Federation.

It has been said that this situation is the result of the British policy of "divide and rule" which separated Singapore from Malaya after the war. The calculation, it is suggested, was that the business rivalry of Kuala Lumpur, the anti-Chinese feelings of the Malays and the ambitions of civil servants could be combined in hostility to Singapore. By this means a sense of unity could be given to the new Federation with anti-Chinese sentiments directed outwards, not inwards, and at the same time Singapore would remain in British hands. It is possible that such ideas were current in some circles; but by itself this interpretation would omit the very real objections on the part of the Malays to the establishment of a state in which they would be a minority.

The economic disadvantages of the separation of Singapore from the peninsula are undeniable, but the situation is not desperate. Singapore by Asian standards is a wealthy city. Its income per head is about twice that of the Federation which itself has one of the highest incomes per head in Asia. There is a considerable and prosperous middle class with a standard of living comparable to most of Europe. There is one car for every thirty people. India, Japan, Indonesia and Pakistan with a population several hundred times larger have only ten times as many cars.

While the economic situation is good, the *entrepôt* trade is subject to fluctuation, and seems to be tending to diminish. At the same time the population of Singapore is increasing at the rate of $3\frac{1}{2}$ per cent a year, and the inhabitants have come to expect a high level of social services. This creates a dilemma. More taxes are required to pay for services; yet taxes may deter foreign investment which is needed for the economy of the island. There has been considerable industrial development, mainly by small-scale enterprises, and the naval base and the Harbour Board play a considerable part in the city's economy. But the main element is the *entrepôt* trade.

The port handles five million tons of cargo a year. The chief exports, or rather re-exports, are rubber and tin, and oil is also important. The trade with the Federation is worth nearly £200 million, £100 million of imports and £88 million of exports. Over and above this, Singapore's trade with other countries amounts to some £700 million a year. Britain spends about £10 million a year in Singapore, and provides grants at the rate of about £100,000 a year. British installations provide employment for nearly 40,000 workers, at wage-levels appreciably higher than the average for the island. If the British were to quit, their departure would have repercussions not only on British interests but also on the population of the island.

Departure is not contemplated by the British Government. In April, 1959, the Minister of Defence, Mr. Duncan Sandys, declared: "There is no doubt about the continuation of the British base in Singapore. It is the pivot of our military situation in the Far East and we have no thought of changing it." The island provides naval, military and air bases. The Royal Navy's Far East Fleet, consisting of one aircraft carrier, one cruiser, four destroyers, four frigates, one despatch vessel and a mine-sweeper squadron, and the Indian Ocean Task Force, consisting of one carrier, one cruiser and one frigate are dependent upon the services it provides. In particular, it has the only dry dock between Sydney and Japan which can take an aircraft carrier. The island affords a military supply base for British forces in Malaya, and for the Commonwealth Strategic Reserve. For the R.A.F. there are three airfields. Moreover, it is the only place in the area where Britain has the right to store nuclear weapons, since British forces in Malaya are not permitted to have them. It is also the only jumping-off point from which military aid may be given to other members of S.E.A.T.O. British forces in Malaya may be used for the defence of Hong Kong, Singapore, Brunei or Malaya itself, but not to help the S.E.A.T.O. countries.

Before the general election in May, 1959, Sir Robert Scott, Commissioner General for south-east Asia and Chairman of the British Defence Co-ordinating Committee for the Far East asserted "A People's Action Party victory would not affect the earlier de-

K 145

cision of the British Government to continue using Singapore as a major naval base for the use of Commonwealth forces." After the election the People's Action Party was in a position to make that policy more difficult; but, in office, the leaders of the P.A.P., with one or two exceptions, have shown themselves to be aware of practical realities. This does not mean that they have dropped all their ideas of anti-colonialism. Their target is integration with the Federation, and to achieve this they recognize that they must make themselves respectable and acceptable. At the same time, they would not wish to take action which would obviously harm the economy of Singapore, and they recognize that the dependence of Singapore on international trade and foreign investment puts special obstacles in the way of pursuing an all-out Socialist pro-gramme.

The P.A.P. Government has not so far raised the question of the continuance of the British base, but this is partly because they appreciate the importance of British spending to the economy of Singapore and partly because they have not been able to achieve integration with the mainland. It is to be expected, however, that to the extent to which they are able to develop Singapore's internal resources and draw closer to the Federation, they will feel freer to challenge the maintenance of the British base. The existing situa-tion may well continue for some years more, and such a continuance is not to be despised or discounted. On the other hand, in the longer run the merger of Singapore with the Federation must be envisaged. Indeed, it is now British policy. In that event, the British base on Singapore would have no greater guarantee of continuance than the Defence Agreement with Malaya, and would not be avail-able in support of S.E.A.T.O. In face of Communist gains in Laos in May, 1962, the British Government decided that, if requested by Siam, they would send a force of R.A.F. fighters from the Singa-pore base. At the same time Tunku Abdul Rahman declared: "The Federation of Malaya will not agree to the Commonwealth forces stationed in Malaya being sent to Thailand in fulfilment of the obligations of the three Commonwealth countries to S.E.A.T.O." If that were to apply to Singapore also, it would involve a re-think-ing and a re-casting of the whole of British and Commonwealth strategy in south-east Asia. It is partly because of that appreciation that attention is being turned to the, as yet, undeveloped possibilities of the British dependencies in Borneo.

II

BORNEO

SARAWAK

IN Borneo the policy of rationalization was more successful than on the Malay peninsula. When the island was occupied by the Japanese there were in its northern part no less than four different régimes. There was, first, Sarawak under British protection and ruled by the third of the Brooke dynasty. Adjacent to it was North Borneo ruled by the British North Borneo Company and also a British protectorate. Embedded in Sarawak was what remained of the Sultanate of Brunei, also protected by Britain—from its neighbours. Finally, the island of Labuan was administered from Singapore.

Sarawak was the first of these territories to receive a new dispensation. Mountbatten ended the period of military administration in April, 1946, and handed back the government to the Rajah. But other plans were in the making. Towards the end of the war the Colonial Office had been considering the question of Sarawak's future relations with Britain and proposed a closer connexion. Although Sarawak was prosperous, there had been a great deal of damage which would be expensive to restore. Aid from Britain would certainly be necessary and Britain would have to control the use of that aid. Moreover, Sarawak was getting out of step with the advance in social welfare and education in other British territories, because its economic development was being deliberately held back by the Rajah in order to prevent foreign exploitation. To obtain revenue for social services fuller use would have to be made of Sarawak's economic resources.

The Rajah too was not unaware of this problem, and after some vacillation decided in October, 1946, to cede the state to the British Crown. The offer was promptly accepted. His main motive seems to have been that he was getting on in years and in poor health, and had no great confidence in his heir; but there was also the argument of the need for economic and technical assistance from Britain which a Labour Government might be reluctant to provide for a country ruled by the Brooke dynasty. Moreover, it was clear that Britain intended to take over North Borneo from the North

Borneo Company, and the contrast of developments in the territory adjoining might well give rise to increasing dissatisfaction in Sarawak. All these reasons contributed to the decision.

The Rajah's private secretary was sent to Sarawak in company with a senior Colonial Office official to obtain the concurrence of the Malay leaders. These proceedings gave rise to similar complaints to those which followed the mission of MacMichael to Malaya—that they had been induced to sign papers which they did not understand. But the Rajah went ahead with the cession. Doubts were raised as to whether the inhabitants of Sarawak approved of the change, and a mission composed of two British Members of Parliament was sent to the country to find out. They reported in favour of the proposal. A Bill was placed before the Council Negri in May, 1946, and achieved a narrow majority. On this basis the British Government decided to go ahead, and on July 1 Sarawak became a Crown colony. The decision did not pass without protest in Sarawak: the most tragic manifestation of opposition was the murder in December, 1948, of the newly appointed Governor. After this climax the country reconciled itself to its new status.

In 1941, just before the Japanese attack the Rajah granted a new constitution to Sarawak. There was scarcely time to put it into operation then, but when Sarawak became a colony the essentials of that constitution were retained, with the Governor replacing the Rajah. There was the Council Negri, a legislative body containing, in addition to officials, a number of members appointed to represent the different peoples and interests in the country, as well as several natives of Sarawak who had served on the previous Council Negri. The executive body was the Supreme Council which was drawn mainly from the Sarawak Civil Service. After ten years came the next stage of political development. A new constitution which took effect at the beginning of 1957 provided for an elected majority on the Legislative Council which has taken the place of the Council Negri. Half of the new Supreme Council is elected from the Legislative Council. Elections to the Legislative Council are indirect, from divisional and municipal councils.

The arrival of politics in Sarawak was signalled in 1959 by the formation of the first political organization, the Sarawak United People's Party. One party leads to another, and a Party Negara has also been formed with mainly Malay membership. That there are also some Communists in Sarawak is not to be doubted, but communalism appears a greater danger at present than Communism. The Sarawak United People's Party has Chinese roots, and consequently has given rise to some nervousness on the part of the indigenous peoples. It is among the Chinese that Communism also has made its appearance. In 1959 the Sarawak Government deported two men to China for Communist agitation: they were alleged to be disseminating revolutionary songs in schools. Secret Communist activity in Sarawak has been traced back to the formation of a Sarawak Overseas Chinese Democratic Youth League in 1951.

If Communism thrives on misery, Sarawak has become less fertile ground. Although there is not necessarily a causal relation, since the territory was ceded to the Crown it has made rapid progress in many spheres. The construction of roads and air-strips has gone ahead. Health services have been improved considerably: malaria has been practically wiped out. Schools have been built. Broadcasting has arrived. Taxes have increased. Generally, civilization is on the march. Sarawak has a five-year plan to spend from 1959 to 1963 M\$ 115 million on agriculture, water supplies, communications, health and education. M\$ 32 million of this will be provided by the U.K. out of the Colonial Development and Welfare Fund. For the remainder Sarawak must look to her own resources.

The three major exports of Sarawak, apart from the Brunei oil which is refined at Lutong and re-exported, are rubber, pepper and timber. Between them these three commodities account for almost four-fifths of the total export earnings of the country. Nearly all the pepper and most of the rubber is exported to Singapore. Half of the timber exports go to the U.K. and most of the rest to Hong Kong or Australia. The re-exports of oil are more widely distributed and it is not possible to be precise about their final destinations, but about a quarter go initially to Singapore, and some to Australia and New Zealand, so that the Commonwealth countries have an overwhelming preponderance in Sarawak's export markets. Imports, apart from the crude oil from Brunei, consist mainly of foodstuffs and consumer goods.

The largest private employer in the country is Sarawak Shell Oilfields Ltd. with a staff of more than 1,500. It holds oil rights over one-fifth of the entire area of Sarawak. Oil was struck at Miri in 1910, and production has subsequently been steady but small in comparison with the output of Brunei. But the Brunei oil also comes through Sarawak via the Lutong refinery. The whole enterprise is a subsidiary of the Royal Dutch Shell Group. Another concern, Sematan Bauxite Ltd., has recently begun mining and exporting aluminium ore. The agency houses are prominent in trading, but less so than in Malaya because the competition from Chinese traders is stronger. But the export of oil and, to a lesser extent, of timber is largely in British hands.

The latest population estimate (1960 census) gives the total number of Europeans as about 1,500 out of a total of about 750,000. The remainder is divided approximately: 236,000 Sea Dayaks, 230,000 Chinese, 175,000 Malay and Melanau, 55,000 Land Dayaks, 37,000 others. It is therefore very much a plural society with all the problems that go with it, particularly in regard to language and education.

The schools could be divided into two types: those in which the medium of instruction was vernacular and English, and those in which the teaching was in Chinese. At the primary level the total number of pupils was divided about equally between the two; but at the secondary level the picture changed and the number of pupils in Chinese-medium schools was markedly greater than the number in English-medium. It is true that English is taught as a subject in the Chinese schools, but this did not alter the fact that there were two systems of education, one in Chinese and one in English, and that the former was tending to predominate.[1]

NORTH BORNEO

The policies for North Borneo and Sarawak reacted upon one another. The liberation of North Borneo involved heavy destruction. Only one building was left standing in Jesselton and none in Sandakan. The cost of rehabilitation was going to be heavy. The board of directors of the North Borneo Company realized that it would be quite beyond their means and so made an approach to the British Government. During the discussions which followed, the future of North Borneo inevitably became associated with plans for Sarawak. From the point of view of development and of adminis-

[1] In an attempt to deal with the problem a Government Ordnance of 1961 required the adoption of English as the common medium of instruction under threat of withdrawal of Government grants. Strong protests came from the Chinese schools, foreshadowing still greater opposition to the eventual adoption of Malay.

strative tidiness it was obviously better that the Crown should take over both territories, and the decision was made accordingly. So North Borneo passed directly from military administration to the status of a Crown Colony on July 15, 1946, without reverting to the North Borneo Company.

Like Sarawak, North Borneo depends for most of its external earnings on three main exports: in this case timber, rubber and copra in that order. The big difference is in the direction of these exports. Whereas Sarawak exports mainly to the U.K. and Commonwealth, Japan is easily the biggest customer of North Borneo. Moreover, while Japan has been increasing her purchases from North Borneo, Britain's share has been declining steadily. Britain still holds first place as the source of North Borneo's imports, but it is not a commanding lead: the U.S.A. and Philippines together supply as much if not more. There is also a large import of oil from Indonesia. Economically, therefore North Borneo is much less Commonwealth-oriented than Sarawak.

The British connexion, however, is very much apparent in the Colonial Development and Welfare grants, amounting to nearly M$ 4 million out of M$ 15 million of development revenue in 1959. Up to 1960 the amount spent or committed by the U.K. in North Borneo under the Colombo Plan was more than £12 million. Experts have been provided and trainees have been sent abroad. In 1957 there were sixty-seven in Australia alone and others elsewhere. The facts of geography make it inevitable and desirable that Australia should take a special interest in the development of North Borneo.

In the private sector the economy is dominated by European concerns engaged in commerce and plantations. In 1959 there were 135 companies incorporated outside the colony and only sixty-three incorporated inside. The largest business house is that of Harrisons & Crosfield with interests in timber and mining, and with agencies for imports, insurance, shipping, air lines, rubber estates, copra and other products. There are other European concerns such as the North Borneo Trading Company which are meeting increasing competition from local Chinese enterprise. But there are no Chinese banks. The Chartered Bank and the Hong Kong & Shanghai have the field to themselves. The European population is mainly employed by these European concerns and exercises economic power in inverse proportion to its size. It was estimated in 1959 at 2,335, including Eurasians, out of a total of over 400,000. Of that total well over half—280,000—were indigenous, and about 100,000 were Chinese; but the latter are increasing at a faster rate.

In 1959 there were about 43,000 children at school of which two-thirds were Chinese, and of the Chinese rather less than half were at mission schools learning English while the majority attended Chinese schools and learned Mandarin. Whereas the product of the mission schools may aspire to a Government job, the children who emerge from the Chinese schools have no such openings, and if they do not find a position with a Chinese employer may well find themselves in the Communist Party. As in Sarawak there is no higher education in North Borneo and students must go overseas. The total of scholarship awards held in 1959 was 150, of which more than half were in Australia and New Zealand under the Colombo Plan. Most of the others also went to Commonwealth countries. Only three went to Japan.

In the administration local recruitment is still at an early stage. The first indigenous District Officer was appointed in 1957, although the majority of Assistant District Officers are now locally recruited.

The Government of the colony, to which the island of Labuan was added in 1946, was at first in the hands of the Governor assisted by an Advisory Council; but in 1950 Executive and Legislative Councils were established. Both have official majorities. There are no elections, and no political parties. Politically North Borneo appears retarded in comparison with Sarawak. The nearest approach to a political organization is represented by the Society of Kedazans headed by Donald Stephens who by birth is part European and part Dusun. Its aim is the social education and economic advancement of the Dusuns, who are the largest indigenous group, in co-operation rather than in competition with the Chinese. It envisages a preparatory period of some fifteen years after which North Borneo would be able to govern itself and resist the Islamic influence coming from Brunei. That expansionism is represented by the Party Ra'ayat led by Azahari who received his political training in Java under Sukarno and the Japanese. The object of this party is a "greater Brunei claiming all the ancient territories", a prospect which does not appeal to the Dusuns of North Borneo who are neither Muslim nor Malays and have inherited memories of Brunei oppression.

BRUNEI

Unlike Sarawak and North Borneo, Brunei remains a protected state. Once it gave its name to the whole island, but it has now been reduced to an enclave of Sarawak. Allied forces returned to Brunei in June, 1945, and the country was under military administration until July of the following year when the Sultan resumed his rule with the assistance of the British Resident.

The Allies and the Japanese had between them done a good deal of damage, the Allies by bombing and the Japanese by setting fire to the Seria oilfields. A glance at the external trade statistics shows that Brunei lives by oil: in 1958 M$ 300 million out of M$ 327 million were earned by export of crude oil. The next most important commodity—rubber—earned only some M$ 2 million. Brunei is therefore very heavily dependent upon oil, and its production is in the hands of the Brunei Shell Petroleum Company Limited. The Company employs nearly 3,000, which is about half the number employed in all the other main sources of occupation—public works, rubber, sawmills, etc. Oil is not only therefore vital to the state's balance of payments; it also dominates the whole economy. Imports are mainly consumer goods, machinery and transport equipment, and in this branch the European agency houses are again prominent.

The estimated population in 1958 was 80,000. The proportion of Chinese in 1947 was 19 per cent and it is thought to have increased since then. In the schools it is considerably higher: in 1958 out of a total of 13,000 enrolled pupils 3,500 were in Chinese schools, and this figure does not include Chinese pupils at mission or Government schools. In the latter the medium of education at the primary level is Malay and at the secondary level English. Students to be trained as teachers are sent to Malaya, Singapore, North Borneo, Sarawak and some to the U.K. For higher education there were in 1958 nearly 100 scholarship-holders distributed between Malaya, Singapore, North Borneo, Sarawak, Australia and the U.K. One-third of them came to the U.K.

The government of Brunei up to 1959 was effectively in the hands of the British Resident, as it had been since the treaty of 1906. His advice had to be asked and acted upon in all matters other than those affecting the Muslim religion. The Resident himself was under the supervision of the High Commissioner who was also the Governor of Sarawak. There was a State Council whose assent was required for legislation. There were also municipal boards; but there were no elections. There was, however, a political party—the Party Ra'ayat mentioned above—and in 1959 there was a new constitution.

In that year the Sultan of Brunei promulgated the first written constitution under which the Brunei State Council was replaced by Executive and Legislative Councils and the post of British Resident was abolished. The Executive Council, over which the Sultan presides, is an appointed body. The Legislative Council is to have almost half of its members elected. At first all of them were nominated, but within two years elections were to be held to District Councils which would, in turn choose the candidates for the Legislative Council.

At the same time, there was an administrative separation of Brunei from Sarawak. The arrangement by which the Governor of Sarawak was simultaneously High Commissioner for Brunei was brought to an end, and a separate High Commissioner was appointed; in fact it was the former British Resident. However, although the personnel remained the same, the constitution was altered. It marked a diminution of British control of the State of Brunei internally and also in the sphere of defence and external affairs. Concurrently, a fresh agreement was made between Britain and Brunei to replace the 1906 agreement in relation to external affairs, defence and internal security and generally on matters other than those affecting the Muslim religion and Malay custom. The High Commissioner has a seat on the Executive Council and the Privy Council, but not on the Legislative Council. The place of the British Resident as head of the Administration has been taken by the Chief Minister.

A significant safeguard was built into the constitution: the consent of the Executive Council is required for any proposal to surrender or cede any part of Brunei or amalgamate, federate or unite any part with another territory. One aspect of this provision looks backward to the history of the successive encroachments upon the territory of Brunei by the adjacent states. The other aspect looks forward to the recurrent suggestion for the "closer association" of Brunei with the other North Borneo territories. This project has obvious attractions in general and for Sarawak and North Borneo in particular. But the attractions are considerably less for the 80,000 people of Brunei who have no public debt, receive a revenue from oil several times greater than their expenditure and could live off the interest from their oversea investments alone. Brunei is the only country in Asia to have a system of old age pensions—and non-contributory at that.

Up to 1959 the policy of "closer association" had official approval. In February of that year the Governor of Sarawak and High Commissioner for Brunei (one and the same) formally proposed that those two territories should, together with British North Borneo, form a central authority to deal initially with defence, external relations, internal security and communications. It was conceived as a single representative of the Crown having as advisers members of the Executive and Legislative Councils of the three territories. The three Governments would continue to control their own revenue and expenditure, but there would be progressive sharing between the territories of other services besides communications, such as trade, customs, banking, currency and research. The arguments in favour of this proposal were that the three territories were small and vulnerable and it was important that they should strengthen their security. There would also be economic advantages deriving from a larger market and cheaper and more efficient trading. However, it met with no response from Brunei, and the constitutional changes which followed soon afterwards, by separating the functions of Governor of Sarawak and High Commissioner, in effect tended in the opposite direction.

Nevertheless, the Governor of North Borneo, while recognizing that the move towards the association of the three territories was blocked because it could not be accomplished without the consent of the peoples concerned, expressed "our continuing goodwill and our desire for such an association". This declaration could hardly have been made unless it were also the policy of the British Government, and in the long run it must be supposed that the proximity of the three territories will bring them together politically. It has been suggested that a beginning might be made with Sarawak and North Borneo, leaving Brunei to stew in its own oil. This would not be a great advance, but it would be a step in the right direction, and others might follow. Even for this limited move, however, the two territories require directly elected representatives to speak for them in the negotiations, and this applies no less to the project of association with Malaya and Singapore. There is therefore a pressing need to hasten the development of representative and responsible self-government. Progress in that direction is being made at a very deliberate speed. In October, 1961, the Government of Sarawak proposed to extend the franchise to adults (over 21) while retaining the system of indirect election and extending the duration of the existing Council Negri to the middle of 1963—by which time Sarawak will hardly have been prepared for entry into a Malaysian federation.

From North Borneo it was reported that steps were being taken towards holding elections, probably about the end of 1962. Meanwhile, the Philippine House of Representatives have urged their Government to lay claim to the territory of North Borneo on behalf of the Philippines as the successor to the Sultan of Sulu, opening a fascinating vista of academic legal argument. Undeterred by this prospect, the British and Malayan Governments have appointed a joint commission, under the chairmanship of Lord Cobbold, to ascertain the views of the people of North Borneo and Sarawak on the question of joining the federation of Malaysia.

12

FURTHER SOUTH AND EAST

IT is ironical that the British made great efforts to re-establish their position in south-east Asia apparently only for the purpose of withdrawing in good order. In 1945 the British returned to Burma, Malaya and Borneo and to territories which had not previously been under British control. Within twelve years they had left Malaya, within three years they had left Burma, and their presence in much of the remaining area was even more short-lived.

The extension of the boundaries of S.E.A.C. from the line of Malaya-Sumatra eastward to New Guinea was as shown above an alteration made abruptly at the time of the surrender. Mountbatten had originally intended to proceed methodically from Malaya to Siam, and thought that he would not be able to undertake operations in Siam before December at the earliest, by which time he hoped the Malayan operation would be finished. He chose Siam rather than Sumatra because of its rice production and because there was already the nucleus of a resistance movement which when armed, supplied and controlled by a mission from S.E.A.C. would be able to render valuable assistance.

SIAM

Britain's interest in Siam focused on the strategic position of the country in relation to south-east Asia, particularly Malaya, and the rice surplus that it was able to supply at a time when there was a serious food shortage in the area as a whole. The Siamese Government, after the entry of Japanese forces, had declared war upon Britain in January, 1942, and had taken advantage of Britain's predicament to occupy the four northern Malay states and the two eastern Shan states in Burma. These territories were added to the other ill-gotten gains which they had made at the expense of Laos and Cambodia. While the Siamese Government was co-operating with and profiting from the Japanese conquests, another group under the exalted patronage of the Regent Pridi began a resistance movement and made contact with the Allies. Promptly on the Japanese surrender, therefore, the Regent was in a position to issue a proclamation denouncing the declaration of war on Britain and stating Siamese readiness to make restitution and to co-operate with the United Nations.

Although the Siamese repudiated their declaration of war, the British Government were not prepared to simply let bygones be bygones, and required the conclusion of a peace treaty. This Agreement was signed on January 1, 1946. Under it Siam agreed to return those parts of Burma and Malaya that it had acquired, to pay compensation for damage to British property in Siam and to permit the resumption of business by British firms. Britain also supported the French claim for the return of those parts of Laos and Cambodia which had been acquired by Siam, and this too was conceded.

The Agreement contained two special features: one, that Siam undertook not to build a canal across the Kra isthmus without the consent of Britain. This proviso represented a constant feature of British policy in south-east Asia ever since the acquisition of Singapore. Having been thrust into Singapore more or less reluctantly by Raffles and having then come to recognize its importance and value, British policy-makers became obsessed by the bogey of a canal through the Kra isthmus which would bypass the gateway to the East. Consequently, Britain seized the opportunity presented at the end of the war to secure a pledge against its construction. Siam was in no position to resist.

The other special feature related to the existence at that time of a general shortage of food in south-east Asia. Siam agreed to make available, without payment, up to 1,500,000 tons of her rice surplus and to offer all further surplus until 1947 for purchase by a special Rice Organization. After the conclusion of the Agreement the rice clauses dominated British relations with Siam. It turned out to be very difficult to extract the rice from the Siamese peasants and merchants and, in the event, only one-tenth of the amount stipulated in the Agreement was supplied free. Siamese peasants wanted something tangible in the way of consumer goods in return for their rice, and the Chinese merchants could, in conditions of scarcity, get a much higher price elsewhere. These provisions of the Agreement were revised after the Special Commissioner for South-East Asia, Lord Killearn, visited Bangkok in 1946, and the British Government undertook to buy 1,200,000 tons of rice at a fixed price over the next twelve months. However, it still proved difficult to obtain the rice and only half the amount was forthcoming. This did not mean that the rice was not exported: large quantities were smuggled into Malaya at much higher prices. In time, as the supply of rice in the area improved and the official price rose, it became more practicable to buy rice from Siam.

The outbreak of Communist terrorism in Malaya augmented British interests in Siam. Britain became concerned first about the asylum afforded to Malayan terrorists across the Siamese border; then about the danger to Siam itself, as well as to the other countries of the area, represented by the Communist victory in China. The British attitude underwent a change from one of reserve towards an ex-enemy country to one of encouragement and co-operation. The outstanding claims for compensation made by Britain and Commonwealth countries were settled by payment of a lump sum of some £5 million by Thailand, and in 1954 the 1946 Agreement was terminated, to be succeeded shortly afterwards by the Manila Treaty which established S.E.A.T.O.

Before the war Britain's interest and influence in Thailand was greater than that of any other power. That position was re-established after the war, partly because Thailand was placed within Mountbatten's area of responsibility, and was maintained until about 1950. Thereafter the U.S.A. began taking greater interest in Thailand, and soon ousted Britain from first place. The volume of British trade with Thailand has remained fairly steady over the past decade at the value of about £15 million a year. The decline in Britain's position is relative to the growth of the U.S. commitment. American aid has been pouring into Thailand, particularly since the creation of S.E.A.T.O., on a scale far beyond the capacity of Britain, and with it American influence has inevitably made a great impact on the country. The British traveller in southern Asia, having passed complacently through the Commonwealth countries of the area without a visa, may be put out to find on arriving in Thailand that he requires a visa but Americans do not.

INDONESIA

The Japanese surrender and the simultaneous extension of Mountbatten's zone of command had repercussions on the orderly progress from Malaya to Thailand which had been envisaged. A rapid adjustment was required: troops had to be sent not only to Siam but to Saigon, Hong Kong and the Indies. A landing had already been effected in June on Labuan and at Brunei by Australian forces, but by the time of the Japanese surrender there had been no penetration into the interior. Three task forces were sent to re-occupy the rest of British Borneo—to Kuching, Jesselton and Sandakan where British administration was re-established by October.

In regard to the Netherlands Indies the instructions to Mount-batten specified two tasks: the despatch of forces to accept the surrender of the Japanese and preparation for the eventual handing over of administration to the Dutch civil authorities. But between the Japanese surrender and the arrival of British forces in any strength an interval of six and a half weeks elapsed. During that time S.E.A.C. was in the position of having to use Japanese troops for administrative and police purposes at long range, and the nationalist movement was able to take over the effective control of the country. Moreover, the British forces, when they arrived at Batavia at the end of September, were mainly composed of Indian units, and it was considered inadvisable to use them for the sup-pression of the nationalist movement. In view of this and having regard to the position established by the Republicans and the strength of the Indonesian hostility to the return of the Dutch, Mountbatten modified the instructions to the forces of liberation. Instead of trying to re-occupy the country they were to limit their efforts to the control of the two key areas of Batavia and Surabaya, collect and disarm the Japanese troops, and rescue the P.O.W.s and internees. Even so, the task was not easy: the control of Surabaya and Semarang had to be secured by force, and the hostility to the Dutch was such that an "Allied" Civil Affairs branch had to be substituted for the Dutch administration. Thus one point of the general policy of restoring the Dutch had to be abandoned under the pressure of circumstances.

Another point—the non-recognition of the nationalist movement —also had to be dropped. The British forces needed local co-operation for the purposes of their own supplies and administra-tion, for rescuing prisoners and internees, and for distributing supplies to the inhabitants. This meant dealing with the Repub-licans and, despite the protests of the Dutch, recognizing *de facto* the Sukarno régime. This was the situation in Java. In the other islands the re-occupation and the return of the Dutch administra-tion went more or less according to plan. But Java was the key to

Indonesia; and this enforced departure from policy on the part of the British led not only to the subsequent war between the Dutch and the Republicans but also to the eventual victory of the latter through their control of the island of Java. It may be said that the course of history was changed by the tactical necessities of the liberating forces and by Mountbatten's method of handling the nationalist movement. For this the Dutch bear the British a grudge, the Indonesians owe some gratitude; but in politics the latter is much more short-lived than the former.

In regard to Indonesia, Britain was in a dilemma: on the one hand, there were obligations towards the Dutch who were her allies and whose sovereign rights over the territories were legally unchallengeable; on the other hand, there was the attitude of the Commonwealth countries in the area who looked to see the emergence of colonial independence. These two expectations were irreconcilable. At first the British Government accepted the Dutch claim but could not give it effect, for the simple reason that Indonesia had been transferred to South-East Asia Command at the last moment and there were not enough troops available to do the job. To supplement British forces it was intended to make use of Japanese troops for police purposes, but this intention was largely frustrated by the Japanese who had generally relinquished control outside Batavia to the Indonesian independence movement. In this situation to take over the country would have required a major military operation, and this was inhibited both by the composition of the British forces and by the desire for demobilization now that the war was over. Such fighting as did occur, at Surabaya and elsewhere in Java, was thrust upon the British by Indonesian action. The policy of the British Government was to try to bring the Indonesians and the Dutch together so as to obtain an agreement.

The actions of the British in Indonesia were raised as a complaint before the Security Council by the Ukraine in January, 1946. The British Foreign Secretary, Mr. Bevin, on February 7, 1946, made a characteristically vigorous defence of British policy: he argued that Dutch sovereignty was incontestable, asserted that the British had been attacked by the extremists, and doubted whether moderate Indonesian leaders wanted British withdrawal at that stage. A senior British diplomat, Sir Archibald Clark Kerr, was sent on a special mission to Batavia in order to try to bring the Dutch and Indonesians together. He succeeded in arranging a meeting between the Indonesian Prime Minister, Sjahrir, and the Dutch Colonial Minister, van Mook. With the arrival of more Dutch forces it became possible for British troops to be withdrawn. The first troops left in March, 1946, somewhat to the dismay of the Indonesian Prime Minister who took the view that the British Army should not leave Java until the political situation was settled. The Indonesians had no great desire to be left *tête-à-tête* with the Dutch.

Relations between the Indonesians and Dutch made little progress, and in August the British Special Commissioner in south-east Asia, Lord Killearn, arrived in Batavia to see whether another attempt could be made to bring them together. In this he was successful and was able to preside at the opening of a conference between the two sides in October. Urgency was added to the need for reaching a settlement because British troops were due to quit Indonesia by the end of November. Before that date agreement was reached at Linggadjati. After the withdrawal of her troops, Britain no longer had direct responsibility for developments in Indonesia but continued the policy of promoting *rapprochement* between the Indonesians and the Dutch and implementation of the Linggadjati Agreement. Later in 1947, however, relations between the two sides again deteriorated, and in July the Dutch began a "police action". This move met with British disapproval. Not merely was there public expression of disappointment but all British military supplies and facilities to the Netherlands in the Far East were suspended. Nevertheless, Britain was reluctant for the dispute to go to the United Nations, taking the view that it was a domestic matter since Britain recognized Dutch sovereignty over Indonesia. It was nevertheless placed on the agenda of the Security Council, and a resolution calling for a cease-fire was proposed on which Britain abstained from voting. Once it had been decided, however, that a committee of good offices was to be established by the United Nations, Britain supported the work of that committee.

When another breach occurred at the end of 1948 between the Indonesians and the Dutch and the latter started a second "police action", the British Government came to the conclusion that a stronger line should be taken; and when the matter came before the Security Council at the end of the year, the British representative supported resolutions calling for the end of hostilities, the release of political prisoners and the resumption of negotiations. Under pressure from Britain and other countries, particularly the United States, the Dutch Government was compelled to yield, and at The Hague Conference in 1949 agreement was reached to transfer sovereignty to a new United States of Indonesia. Britain welcomed this outcome and, when the new state was established at the end of the year, quickly extended recognition.

Relations between Britain and Indonesia subsequently tended to decline. Trade between the two countries reached its peak in 1951 and since then has fluctuated between £20 million and £30 million a year, with on the whole a downward trend. British concerns in Indonesia have suffered from the inability of the Indonesian Government to make up its mind whether the national revolution demanded the elimination of foreign *entrepreneurs* or encouragement of foreign investment. In 1959 British concerns included two major banks, tyre, soap and margarine plants, and tobacco and rubber estates. The renewal of leases on rubber estates had run into difficulties, and the imposition of a 20 per cent levy on remittances from Indonesia was not encouraging. On the other hand, Indonesia joined the Colombo Plan in 1953 and since then has received more than £250,000 of technical aid from Britain. After a period of embargo Britain has resumed the sale of arms to Indonesia.

The embargo was imposed in consequence of Indonesian claims and threats against "West Irian"—Western New Guinea—the sole remnant of the Dutch empire in the East. The Indonesian argument is that as part of the former Netherlands East Indies it should have been handed over to Indonesia. Other countries, unimpressed by the capacity of the Indonesian Government to administer the islands which it holds, do not appreciate the desirability of the transfer. This is particularly the case of Australia which is responsible for the other half of New Guinea. The consideration which Britain owes to Holland as a N.A.T.O. ally has therefore been strengthened by the interest of the Commonwealth country most directly affected. Australia's concern arises from doubts about the desirability of Indonesia as a neighbour. Partly as a result of the ill-advised Dutch policy after the war, the character of the Indonesian régime retains a strongly anti-foreign tinge and would-be revolutionary colouring. Indonesia has the largest Communist Party in Asia outside China and the régime to some extent leans upon it for support.

The political character of Indonesia concerns also her other

Commonwealth neighbours—Malaya, Singapore and British Borneo. Looking ahead it is possible to envisage Indonesia laying claim to British Borneo in the same way as to West Irian on irredentist grounds. Moreover, the language of Indonesia is a variant of Malay, and the Malays are kindred people. The vision of a united Malaysia combining the peninsula with the archipelago evokes a response. But it is difficult to conceive of it being led by any country other than Indonesia which is by far the biggest in area and population; and that prospect, on the basis of Indonesia's performance hitherto, cannot be contemplated with equanimity.

INDO-CHINA

The pattern of events in Indo-China was similar. There too, between the Japanese surrender and the arrival of British forces, a hiatus occurred; but in this case it was not the British responsibility to return the territory to French control—the French preferred to attend to that themselves. The first British troops, commanded by Major-General Gracey, were flown into Saigon a month after the surrender, by which time the Viet Minh had established themselves both in the north and in the south of Vietnam and were proclaiming an independent republic. Although it was not his intention nor in his directive, Gracey felt increasingly obliged, in the interests of the safety of his troops and of French civilians, to extend the sphere of his authority against that of the Viet Minh. This extension received the approval of the Chiefs of Staff, although Mountbatten advised against it, and Gracey was authorized to assist the French to maintain order outside the key areas in Vietnam south of the 16th parallel. Under his auspices a truce was concluded between the French and the Viet Minh at the beginning of October; but when it proved ineffectual owing to violations by the Viet Minh he determined to occupy the whole of Saigon, instead of a few key points, and to exercise full control in conjunction with the French civil administration. This required some hard fighting in which the Japanese troops helped the British. There followed a build-up of French forces and in January 1946 Gracey handed over to Admiral Thierry D'Argenlieu.

The chief difference in the British situation in Indo-China as compared with Indonesia was that, unlike the Dutch, the French had forces available at a fairly early stage for the purpose of re-establishing their administration. They were able to take over the administration in the British zone of operations early in October, 1945, and consequently, the question of extending *de facto* recognition to the nationalist movement did not arise. Towards the end of 1945 British troops began to leave the country and at the beginning of 1946 there was an Anglo-French agreement under which the French were in future to maintain law and order in southern Indo-China, with the exception of a few places where the Japanese forces were interned for repatriation. At the end of January, 1946, Saigon itself was transferred to the French and in March Indo-China ceased to be under South-East Asia Command. In consequence of this relatively early evacuation the British were able in Indo-China to avoid any major involvement in the conflict between the returning French and the nationalist movement which only came to a head after the British had left. Nevertheless, British policy in relation to this situation was similar to the policy pursued in Indonesia, that is, to encourage both sides to reach a compromise. The withdrawal of British troops freed Britain from involvement in the conflict but also deprived her of a lever for the exercise of influence.

Developments in Indo-China followed a course contrary to the policy pursued in British territories. While the demands of the nationalist movements in British India, Burma and Ceylon were met by rapid progress towards self-government, the evolution of Indo-China was marked by continuous warfare and concessions grudgingly extracted, too little and too late. The British view of the conflict in Indo-China was divided between suspicion of the Communist domination of the nationalist movement and sympathy for the national aspirations of the people. In 1949, however, the success of the Communists in China put a different aspect on the situation. It posed with special urgency the problem of the strategic defence of south-east Asia, particularly Malaya. Whereas previously British policy had been one of encouraging an agreement between France and the nationalists, henceforward British policy was concerned with the danger of Chinese domination of the region. Consequently, Britain began to view the Bao Dai régime with greater interest as a possible alternative to a Viet Minh victory. The Commissioner-General in south-east Asia, Mr. Malcolm MacDonald, visited Indo-China in November of that year bringing a message of support from the Foreign Minister. As soon as the French agreement with Bao Dai was ratified in 1950, Britain extended recognition to his Government and also to Laos and Cambodia as associated states within the French Union.

It was Britain's recognition of the Peking Government that gave her the position of co-chairman at the Geneva Conference in 1954. At a conference in which Communist China was a participant, the U.S.A. could not lead the Western powers and France was too heavily involved in Indo-China. Britain's ability at the time of the Indo-China crisis to play a mediatory role, which contributed to the agreement then reached, was a vindication of the policy of recognizing Peking. But more was at stake than the prestige of presiding over an important international conference. Apart from the general interest of avoiding a major conflict Britain had a special interest in the Geneva negotiations. Sir Anthony Eden has recorded: "My chief concern was for Malaya. I wanted to ensure an effective barrier as far to the north of that country as possible."

Similar considerations are to be seen in the British reaction to the American proposal for a collective defence organization. The British assessment of the situation in Vietnam differed from the American. Whereas the State Department seemed to hold the view that the position could still be saved by threat of Western intervention, Eden believed that any negotiated settlement was bound to produce either Communist participation in the government of the whole of Vietnam or partition, and that the latter was preferable. He felt, therefore, that to form and announce a military coalition before the conference would not help and might do harm by alienating potential supporters. But a collective defence arrangement following the conference would be another matter: he welcomed it because it "would contribute to the security of Malaya and Hong Kong and would remove the anomaly of our exclusion from the A.N.Z.U.S. Pact" which had been concluded in 1951 between the U.S.A., Australia and New Zealand.

Since the Geneva Conference Britain has played a larger part in the problems of Indo-China than her direct interests would seem to warrant. Any renewal of tension, as in Laos in 1960–2, is likely to call for a resumption of the position of co-chairman of the conference. This leading diplomatic role is not matched in other spheres. Britain shares the general S.E.A.T.O. commitments; and also has a particular interest in the Commonwealth countries in the neighbourhood. But, strategy apart, in Indo-China itself Britain has very little stake. Her annual trade with Cambodia, Laos and South

Vietnam amounts to £2–£3 million a year. In South Vietnam America's weight is heavily preponderant. The desire to replace French by English as the second language has furthered the spread of American influence. But the eagerness to acquire some knowledge of the English language in one or other of its versions affords an opportunity for developing links with Britain, especially as there is a tendency to seek a counterbalance to American predominance.

PRESENT AND FUTURE

13

AID AND TRADE

"The English language is widely in use throughout the world as the language of education, administration, culture and technology. And its use is growing. This fact is both a source of pride and an avenue of opportunity. Our language is, so to say, a window through which our country and its people can be seen —provided there are available the teachers, the facilities for the teaching of teachers, the books and periodicals which are needed to sustain and where possible to increase its use."

So runs a Government White Paper published in 1959. The conclusion drawn was that the overseas information services needed to be strengthened, and it was decided to increase the amount spent on them—by £1½ million. The cost overall was to go up from £15 million to £16½ million, part of which would be available for south-east Asia.

The conclusion was right but the reasons were wrong. The English language was regarded merely as a means of presenting Britain to other countries, and the desire of foreigners to acquire it was represented as an opportunity to disseminate propaganda. This approach is likely to be self-defeating if it gives the recipients the impression that they are being "got at". In south-east Asia people are specially sensitive on this point and are disposed to resist anything that savours of cultural colonialism just as much as economic or political imperialism. More benefit would be derived all round from a different approach by which the provision of facilities for acquiring a knowledge of English is regarded as a method of aiding development. English is valued as a means of access to knowledge of the sciences and arts of the wider world. In the process of acquiring it, Asian students are bound to encounter Britain's contribution which is likely to be understood better by this means than by propagandist efforts to "sell" Britain to them.

In providing facilities for learning English the role of the British Council is important. In 1959–60 it spent rather more than £5 million. Of that amount rather less than £200,000 was spent in south-east Asia and the Far East. The annual report records that a British Council representative was posted to Saigon—a new departure—and that lecturers in English were recruited for Vietnam, Cambodia and Laos and arrangements made for the supply of books, periodicals and English teaching materials. Lecturers were appointed to train English teachers at the training college in Rangoon and to organize a linguistics department at the University of Mandalay. In Indonesia an additional lecturer in English was appointed to Djakarta and funds were made available for books. In Thailand an English language specialist was seconded to the Ministry of Education and seven teachers were recruited to work in schools or training colleges.

This represents one year's expansion of activity. It omits the facilities and staff already provided—libraries, representatives, lecturers—and it does not include Malaya and Singapore where English is well entrenched in the educational system. The Government of Malaya even maintains two colleges in the U.K. for the training of teachers. How long they will survive is uncertain. Pride and economy may soon bring them to an end. Before that happens it is to be hoped that the British Government will step in. The maintenance of those two colleges would be an extremely valuable investment for Britain. Indeed, there is a strong case for providing similar facilities for students from other countries also.

Britain's cultural relations with the non-Commonwealth countries of the region are on an altogether minor scale. Personnel supplied by the British Council range in number from two each for the countries of Indo-China to twenty or more in Indonesia. To these services should be added the contribution of the Overseas Service of the B.B.C. and the facilities provided by the Central Office of Information. In addition there are the information services of the British missions abroad attached to the High Commissions, Embassies or Legations in the various countries. Yet, taking all these into account, the total resources employed on education in south-east Asia are meagre.

It is important, however, to avoid the fallacy of numbers. A common reaction to the problem of aid to under-developed countries is to find out how much Britain is giving and ask for more. There is much to be said for the spirit of this response, and something to be said for it in practice as the needs of those countries are so vast and the temptation for Governments to restrict contributions is strong. But it does not follow that an increase in expenditure on these activities would produce correspondingly improved results. Much depends on the quality of the personnel recruited for this work, and the resources of Britain in that respect are not unlimited. Nevertheless there is no doubt that more could be done if it were regarded as important enough to warrant the increased expenditure.

In recent years the trend has been upwards, and there has been a welcome innovation by the allocation of funds to subsidize British books for sale abroad. In 1959 the Norrington Committee on the selection of low-priced books for overseas was set up to advise on the works that should be chosen for sale abroad below cost. It was estimated that the amount of the subsidy would run to about £500,000 a year. The object was two-fold. The immediate aim was to meet the competition of subsidized literature produced by other countries, particularly the Communist *bloc*. Non-English-speaking countries have long taken advantage of the prevalence of English in Asia as a medium for disseminating their ideology. The Norrington Committee was a step in the direction of providing alternative literature at a price within reach of students. It is easier to provide propaganda, but self-defeating in the long run. Copies of English classics and textbooks are more effective than expositions of the "British way of life" because they meet a real need.

One of Britain's major contributions to the development of south-east Asia has been made through the Colombo Plan which was launched at a meeting of Commonwealth Foreign Ministers in Ceylon in 1950. A committee was set up to assess the needs of southern Asia and survey the resources available to meet them. The Commonwealth countries in the area agreed to draw up six-year development programmes and the countries outside the area announced the contributions they would make. Arrangements for technical co-operation were worked out, and other countries were invited to join. During the first period of operation, all the non-Commonwealth countries of south-east Asia, except North Vietnam, decided to participate, and so did the U.S.A. This success encouraged the extension of the Colombo Plan, first to 1961, then to 1966, with further prolongation envisaged. Britain, as one of the donor countries, has provided substantial economic and technical aid. Under the latter head the total amount spent by Britain up to 1960 in south-east Asia amounted to about £1½ million.

(This figure does not include aid given by Britain from the Colonial Development and Welfare Funds which is on a much greater scale: in the year 1959–60 the allocations from that source to Singapore, North Borneo and Sarawak amounted to £7 million.) The number of student trainees who came to the U.K. during that period was 858,[1] the number of experts provided was 63.[2] Some of the money has been spent on the supply of equipment such as books for science teaching in Burma or apparatus for the Forest Products Research Institute of Cambodia. Among the recipients of this type of aid are such varied institutions as the Motor Mechanics' Training Centre at Vientiane in Laos, the Science Teachers' Training Centre at Bandung in Indonesia, the Chulalongkorn Hospital Training Centre in Thailand, and the Agricultural Research Station in Kachin State, Burma. Britain is committed to provide £9 million for technical assistance under the Colombo Plan up to 1963 of which about half had been used by 1960.

The Government's recent decision to set up a Department of Technical Co-operation is a recognition both that the work is important and that it is going to continue. The new departure does not by itself mean any increase in outlay—its budget will be about £25 million—but it will take over and co-ordinate the work in this field which has hitherto been divided between three other departments—the Foreign Office, the Colonial Office and the Commonwealth Relations Office. The Department began to operate in July, 1961, with its work distributed between three divisions. The first had the task of selecting and preparing officers for the Overseas Service, and also those sent to Britain from overseas for training courses. The second was to cover social services, students and research, and the provision of technical assistance. The third was to be responsible for finance and relations with the U.N. and other international organizations and also with other countries that are supplying aid. The Department is intended to channel technical assistance where it is most required. It is not restricted to aid from Government sources, but will deal with professional bodies, business, universities and scientific organizations. It should mean more

[1] One hundred and one from Malaya, 233 from Burma, 170 from Indonesia, 139 from Thailand, 24 from Laos, 12 from Vietnam, 8 from Cambodia and 171 from the Philippines.

[2] Ten from Malaya, 21 for Burma, 15 for Indonesia, 3 for Laos, 4 for Thailand, 6 for Vietnam and 4 for Cambodia.

effective use of available resources and a more coherent pattern for Britain's contribution.

Economic aid to the countries of south-east Asia has been a considerably larger item. Capital supplied to the British Commonwealth territories in the area up to 1960 amounted to £65 million with further commitments of £13 million. The projects for which this money has been used include the new international airport at Paya Lebar on Singapore, an east-west road and a new technical college in Malaya, and hospitals and roads in North Borneo and Sarawak. There was also help given to other countries belonging to the Colombo Plan bringing the total of aid and technical assistance for the period in south and south-east Asia to something approaching £150 million.

In addition there has been private investment in under-developed countries running at the rate of about £100 million a year, part of which has been channelled to south-east Asia. Just how much this amounts to for the area as a whole cannot be determined precisely; but figures are available for Burma, Malaya, Singapore and Indonesia which before the Second World War accounted for most of the British investment in south-east Asia. As is to be expected, the estimates for those countries show a decline during the war, and the trend continued in the post-war period. From 1946 to 1956 the total dropped by £4 million. This trend contains two contrary movements—disinvestment in Burma and Indonesia, and increased investment in Malaya and Singapore—but the rate of withdrawal has been higher than the influx of capital.

The total of Government aid and private investment to underdeveloped countries by Britain since the war adds up to approximately £2,500 million. On this reckoning the share of south-east Asia has constituted only a small portion. One comparison may be cited by way of illustration. In 1958 the amount of aid provided by the U.K. to the countries covered by S.E.A.T.O. was less than $5½ million; in the same period the amount of U.S. aid to the same countries was $340 million.

There has been trade as well as aid. The volume of trade between Britain and south-east Asia in recent years is shown in the accompanying table. The striking feature of it is the pre-eminence of Singapore and the predominance of Singapore taken with Malaya. But that feature is only notable in comparison with the trade with the other countries of the region. As the table shows, the sum total

Year	Malaya		Singapore		Borneo		Burma	
	Imports	Exports	Imports	Exports	Imports	Exports	Imports	Export
1947	17·5	12·3	12·3	18·0	0·6	1·3	3·6	20·5
1948	17·4	16·5	14·9	20·5	1·3	2·3	6·1	14·1
1949	13·9	19·0	11·8	23·3	1·2	3·0	3·2	7·1
1950	36·7	24·0	21·3	30·1	2·6	3·1	2·6	9·0
1951	91·5	40·0	53·6	47·9	6·3	3·5	5·6	11·9
1952	60·3	41·0	39·5	45·6	5·5	4·4	9·9	15·3
1953	33·5	33·4	25·8	38·3	6·3	5·6	8·1	20·0
1954	27·5	30·9	24·7	35·2	9·9	5·5	7·1	22·9
1955	47·6	36·0	37·6	38·5	10·7	5·3	8·2	22·0
1956	42·9	40·4	34·4	42·0	12·9	5·6	7·8	17·4
1957	44·0	38·8	26·4	40·0	9·1	4·5	7·8	21·8
1958	40·3	35·4	20·2	36·3	9·5	4·8	6·9	11·8

of that trade does not bulk large in the picture of Britain's commerce. Although the figures as compared with the inter-war period are much bigger, their proportion of the total is not much altered, fluctuating between 3 per cent and 4 per cent.

In 1961 a delegation sponsored by the Board of Trade and the Federation of British Industries visited the countries of southeast Asia. Their report, published under the title "A Trade in Transition", presented a bleak picture. For the most part the transition appears to be in a downward direction. British exports to Burma between 1956 and 1960 fell from 20 per cent to 14 per cent and Britain lost first place to Japan as Burma's supplier. This may be accounted for in part by the payment of reparations from Japan, but that cannot apply to the U.S.A. or to China who also made inroads into the Burma trade. The decline was to be seen also in exports to Malaya and Singapore: alone of the major exporting countries Britain's share dropped by 16 per cent. Exports to Indonesia also declined—by more than 12 per cent—but so did those of every other country except China. In the case of Sarawak, however, British exports diminished while Japan, Indonesia and West Germany increased their trade.

There was an improvement in British exports to some countries. The amount sent to Thailand increased by some 4 per cent; but West German exports rose by more than 30 per cent and Japanese by more than 50 per cent. The quantity of British exports to North

Thailand		Indo-China		Indonesia		S.E.A.	Grand Total
ports	Exports	Imports	Exports	Imports	Exports	Total	
0·6	1·6	—	0·9	1·0	5·7	95·9	2,993
1·2	2·8	—	1·0	1·9	8·5	108·5	3,724
3·0	4·7	0·1	0·7	7·1	12·6	110·7	4,119
3·8	6·9	0·4	0·7	12·7	8·6	162·5	4,864
3·0	11·4	1·9	0·7	32·0	13·1	319·4	6,610
1·0	14·5	0·5	1·7	12·4	17·0	268·6	6,205
1·0	14·3	0·1	2·8	7·0	14·1	210·3	6,030
2·6	11·6	0·4	1·5	8·8	10·2	198·8	6,147
2·5	12·3	1·6	1·5	11·3	11·4	246·5	6,905
3·0	13·7	0·6	2·3	10·0	16·1	249·1	7,204
2·8	12·5	0·3	2·7	10·0	13·4	234·1	7,528
3·7	11·9	0·6	2·1	10·9	7·6	202·0	7,130

Borneo increased much more—by 36 per cent—but almost every other supplier showed a faster rate of growth. There was a similar rise in British exports to the Philippines; but in the cases where British trade increased the amount involved was relatively small. Taking the area as a whole, British exports declined by £14 million between 1955 and 1959, while imports into the area rose by £18 million. So far from Britain improving her position, she was failing to keep pace with her competitors.

The picture of Britain's relations with south-east Asia in the cultural and economic fields shows a decline from her position of ascendancy during the inter-war period. Britain could not be expected to endure the experience of crushing defeat at the hands of the Japanese and the economic debilitation of the war against the Axis, and emerge unscathed. That Britain's position at the end of the war should have been much inferior to what it was at the beginning is not to be wondered at. But since the end of the war there has been a further decline. The ending of the Empire in the East, of which Singapore and Borneo are the only surviving remnants in south-east Asia, has been a contributory factor. It may be argued that the new relationship established with the independent Commonwealth countries offset the breaking of the old colonial ties, and to some extent this argument is valid. It is generally true that the new relationship of equality is healthier and more cordial, but that does not make it closer. On the contrary, the independent

M

Commonwealth countries now have the opportunity to choose their friends from a wider circle and are less dependent on Britain; and this is still more true of Burma which has left the Commonwealth.

Added to this loosening of the Commonwealth connexion is the factor of Britain's relative economic decline. The U.K. has lost the place that she held in the inter-war period, being progressively outdistanced by the U.S.A., the U.S.S.R. and by the developing European Economic Community. The economic relations of Britain with south-east Asia have not changed much but those of other countries have: in particular the U.S.A. has achieved much greater standing and influence, Japan has resumed her economic penetration and the Soviet Union has also been carving out a share. The Foreign Languages Publishing House in Moscow has issued in English, at a price which British subsidized sales would find difficult to match, a book on *Soviet Trade with South-East Asia* in which the point is made that "There is a direct link between the political relations of states and their commercial relations". This is true for Britain also: the decline in her economic position has political repercussions.

There are, however, certain assets which can be utilized. One of them is the Commonwealth connexion which, although more tenuous, still exists and exercises an influence. The activities of Britain in developing cultural relations have been indicated and more could be done in that direction. Non-governmental organizations, like the British Association of Malaya, are doing valuable work in maintaining the British connexion, mainly from the British end; but the deficiency is greater on the Asian side. Perhaps the most successful of the British contributions in the economic field has been the launching of the Colombo Plan; but, although Britain provided much of the impetus, its continuance is dependent upon other countries.

Given the limited resources of these islands Britain must reconcile herself to playing a lesser role on the south-east Asian stage. Hopes may be cherished that the peoples of south-east Asia, reacting from American or Russian predominance, will look to Britain as an arbiter; but they are illusory. The chief reason why Britain is relatively more popular in south-east Asia now than she was between the wars is precisely because she has lost the position of ascendancy. The Americans who have taken it over have also incurred the odium which then attached to Britain. If Britain were to revive her dominant position in the area the old ill-feeling would revive with it. However, this is out of the question. In the provision of personnel, facilities, and economic aid Britain could not, even if she wished, compete with America. But she could obviously increase the amount of resources which she now devotes to south-east Asia if it was thought worthwhile.

The general importance of the area has grown with the emergence of Communist China. The Chinese Revolution has turned south-east Asia into a borderland where the Communist and non-Communist worlds meet. Consequently it has become an area of potential Communist advance which has to be contained. Britain has a general interest in limiting the expansion of Communism in south-east Asia as elsewhere, and a special position as a result of the Geneva Conference. This is one reason for Britain making a contribution towards the economic stability and development of the region.

There is also Britain's particular interest arising out of her commitments to the Commonwealth countries in the area and the benefits which are derived from them. On these grounds some extra effort might be expected. The reason that it has not been made is primarily because, ever since her repulse by the Dutch in the seventeenth century, Britain has been more interested in India than in the Indies. This is still true today. If there is a choice of allocating scarce resources between the Indian sub-continent and south-east Asia the requirements of the former will prevail. It is difficult to quarrel with this assessment of the relative importance of those two regions. The maintenance of India as a bastion of democracy in southern Asia is a concept which receives general endorsement and support. It is not so clearly recognized that the success or failure of the Indian development may turn upon events in south-east Asia.

The area is intrinsically important because it lies strategically across major lines of communication and produces valuable commodities for the world market. Most of the world supplies of Manila hemp, natural rubber, copra, coconut oil, tin and rice for international trade are drawn from south-east Asia. The loss of them would be serious; but the Second World War showed that diverting those supplies and cutting the lines of communication would not necessarily be decisive. The area has still greater significance from another aspect. As the name Indo-China indicates, it has for centuries been the meeting ground of two civilizations. Precisely because that is where the economic and cultural contest is being fought in close proximity to the Communist sphere, it warrants more attention than it has hitherto received from Britain. What is at stake is in the first instance the survival of the independent countries of the area. On that depends the position of the Indian sub-continent—on which, in turn, hinges the global struggle of the two worlds.

14

STRATEGY AND POLITICS

THE first impression of relations between the West and south-east Asia is one of a multiplicity of organizations duplicating and overlapping. The impression is not dispelled by closer inspection. A glance at the 1961 S.E.A.T.O. report illustrates the point: the organization was not confined to military matters, but also indulged in economic and cultural activities. Under its economic activities are listed the Graduate School of Engineering, in Bangkok; skilled labour projects for the supply of trained man-power in Thailand, Philippines and Pakistan; cholera research and a general medical research project; a conference on community de-velopment; and a scheme for meteorological aviation telecom-munications (in other words, weather reporting). All these are no doubt good works, but it is difficult to see how they differ from the kind of activity carried out under the Colombo Plan or by bilateral arrangements.

Similarly the S.E.A.T.O. Cultural Relations programme appears to be doing what is already being done. It provides undergraduate scholarships, post-graduate studentships, research fellowships and professorships for educational co-operation and cultural contact; and it has sponsored conferences and particular projects such as the compilation and publication of a descriptive catalogue of ancient Arabic, Persian and Urdu manuscripts. These too are no doubt admirable activities, but again it may be asked how they differ from other programmes for the provision of technical aid, and also how they are related to the purposes of S.E.A.T.O.

Here the ambiguity in S.E.A.T.O. is encountered. When the organization was established in 1954 it was in response to the crisis in Vietnam, and its main object was to draw the line against the advance of Communism in south-east Asia just as N.A.T.O. had done in Europe. But there was also a hazy notion that military containment was not enough. It was necessary to provide security against a direct Communist assault; but Communism could also expand by permeation and penetration, and to meet this danger the best precaution was to strengthen the economic and social structures of the countries in the area. So article 3 was written into the Manila Treaty :

> "The Parties undertake to strengthen their free institutions and to co-operate with one another in the further development of economic measures, including technical assistance, designed both to promote economic progress and social well-being and to further the individual and collective efforts of Governments towards these ends."

"Free institutions" in this context has to be interpreted freely. It must mean "non-Communist" or "independent", for it could hardly be said that Thailand enjoyed free institutions in the sense of "liberal" or "democratic", and the democracy of Pakistan was superseded by the dictatorship of Ayub Khan. That S.E.A.T.O. was directed against Communism is implicit in the treaty and made explicit by America's reservation that her guarantee applied only to Communist aggression. The double-talk about "free institutions" has been a weakness inherent in the organization from its inception.

The root of this ambiguity is understandable. It arises from the idea that anti-Communism is not enough. There is a desire to have a positive, not merely a negative, aim. The economic and cultural activities of S.E.A.T.O. directed towards that object are valuable in themselves. They do not actually duplicate what is being done under the Colombo Plan, for they are additional. But they are of the kind that, in the absence of S.E.A.T.O., might have been covered by the Colombo Plan—or might not. All the Asian members of S.E.A.T.O. have also joined the Colombo Plan; it is understandable that they should expect to derive some additional benefit from their adherence to the Manila Treaty. The main benefit is military protection; but in view of the nature of the antagonist a case can be made for some economic and cultural supplement. But only as a supplement. By itself it would be absurdly inadequate. It only begins to make sense when taken in conjunction with the total supply of aid to the area from all sources.

If the economic and cultural activities of S.E.A.T.O. are marginal what of its main function? In addition to resisting Communist penetration it was designed to prevent Communist expansion either by aggression or by subversion. The latter technique was expressly dealt with in Article 2 of the treaty :

"The Parties, separately and jointly, by means of continuous and effective self-help and mutual aid will maintain and develop their individual and collective capacity to resist armed attack and to prevent and counter subversive activities directed from without against their territorial integrity and political stability."

The problem of subversion from without is undoubtedly a real one, but it cannot be said that this provision makes any great contribution towards dealing with it. "Aggression", which is apparently straightforward enough, has been notoriously difficult to define: but in comparison with the task of delimiting "subversion" it is child's play. The pragmatist's answer to the problem of determining aggression is to compare it with an elephant: you may not be able to define an elephant but you know it when you see it. But even this will not serve in the case of subversion: it may not be immediately recognizable. In the Laos crisis of 1960, for example, was there civil war or subversion from without? The answer depends on an estimate of the relations between the Left-wing faction and the Viet Minh, which could not be known for certain. The S.E.A.T.O. Council in March, 1961, "noted with grave concern the continued offensive by rebel elements in Laos who are continuing to be supplied and assisted by Communist powers" and declared their readiness to take appropriate action if there continued to be "active military attempts to obtain control of Laos". It also pointed to "the efforts of an armed minority, again supported from outside in violation of the Geneva Accord, to destroy the Government of Vietnam, and declared its firm resolve not to acquiesce in any such takeover of that country". In both cases it took the view that there was subversion, as was highly probable; but for other countries outside the Communist *bloc* that pronouncement might not suffice and they might well take a different view.

In a case of aggression S.E.A.T.O. is on firmer ground. It may be said that the organization is best equipped to deal with the least likely danger, because aggression is much less probable than subversion. If so, it is a testimonial; for it is surely the existence of S.E.A.T.O. which helps to make aggression unlikely. It contributes two things: a form of guarantee and a degree of military coordination.

The guarantee is to be found in Article 4 of the treaty:

"Each Party recognizes that aggression by means of armed attack

183

in the treaty area against any of the Parties, or against any State or territory which the Parties by unanimous agreement may hereafter designate, would endanger its own peace and safety, and agrees that it will in that event act to meet the common danger in accordance with its constitutional processes."

This form of words may be contrasted with the undertaking in the North Atlantic Treaty where there is no proviso about constitutional processes. In practice the response to an act of aggression might be similar in either case, but the wording of the Manila Treaty contains a suggestion of less immediacy.

The military co-ordination under S.E.A.T.O. reinforces this interpretation. There is nothing comparable to the integration of forces in the West under a supreme allied commander. The organization is directed by a Council of Ministers which normally meets only once a year, but in the interval their Representatives meet frequently—forty-eight times in 1960. These bodies have expert committees to advise them and a secretariat in Bangkok to carry out the civilian work of the organization. Its military activities are directed by military advisers from each member country, and there is a Military Planning Office in Bangkok headed by an Australian general. Combined exercises are performed periodically, but the forces are not under a unified command.

There is, however, some integration of the Commonwealth contribution. Co-ordinated defence planning was begun by Britain, Australia and New Zealand in 1949 for the area referred to as A.N.Z.A.M. comprising British territories in Malaya and Borneo and the adjacent waters. There was no firm commitment by Australia and New Zealand for the defence of Malaya until 1955 when they agreed to station military units there. The U.S.A. and France were associated with defence arrangements in the area by means of a five-power Staff Agency set up in 1953, which was superseded by S.E.A.T.O.

The Commonwealth strategic reserve for south-east Asia is stationed at a new base near Malacca which was opened in August, 1960. The cost of it—£7 million—was met by the U.K., Australia and New Zealand, and the main component of the forces there is the 28th Commonwealth Infantry Brigade. Yet these troops are not available directly for the purposes of S.E.A.T.O. Tunku Abdul Rahman made this clear in connexion with the Laos crisis in April,

1961. He confirmed that he had been approached about the movement of troops if war arose over Laos, and his answer was that the
troops might be removed after due notice but "they cannot use this
country as a base for stationing troops and moving them from here
to the battlefront. If they want the troops they can remove them
for good. We will not be party to any war or power struggle. If
there is trouble in Singapore, Hong Kong or Borneo then we are
in it, but not when any S.E.A.T.O. country is involved in war."
This limitation applies equally to the main air base used by the
Commonwealth units in Malaya at Butterworth. Hence there is
increased interest in the potentialities of Borneo. But the facilities
available there are not comparable. For Britain the key to strategy
in south-east Asia is still, as it has been for over a century, Singapore.

Singapore is the largest British naval base outside the U.K. and
a considerable portion of Britain's naval strength operates from it.
The force now includes a commando carrier as a base for Royal
Marine Commandos. So the strength which can be mustered from
the Singapore base in an emergency amounts to one aircraft carrier,
the commando carrier, a cruiser and a handful of destroyers,
frigates and minesweepers. In comparison with the American
Seventh Fleet which amounts to about 130 vessels including several
carriers, cruisers with guided missiles and nuclear submarines it is
not a very significant element in the defences of the area, although
it is a useful addition. Any realistic assessment of the defences of
south-east Asia must recognize that the safety of the area from any
major aggression is dependent on American striking-power.

The British contribution is a wasting asset. A great deal of
money has been poured into the Singapore base—its cost is estimated as at least £100 million a year—but its future is in doubt.
Assuming that the political development of Singapore will be in
the direction taken by Malaya its use is likely to be restricted. If
Britain and Singapore fail to agree on the next steps, its facilities
are liable to be curtailed because it is dependent upon local labour
which is highly susceptible to political pressures. Nor are the forces
stationed in the East likely to increase. On the contrary, the trend is
the other way. In 1958 Britain had six infantry battalions stationed
in the Far East; in 1961 there were four, and the Government were
considering further reductions. The economic cost of a strategy
which involves maintaining a "military presence" in far-flung

quarters of the globe is proving too heavy. There is increasing attraction in the alternative policy of creating a really strong strategic reserve with transport aircraft to move it quickly wherever required. The effectiveness of the American Seventh Fleet lends strength to this argument, by demonstrating the advantages of flexibility. Churchill once described Singapore as a "battleship without a bottom"; but an immobile battleship is not much use for naval operations.

The force of circumstances is pressing for a diminution of Britain's strategic role in the East. To those who lament the surrender of Britain's leading position, achieved over the centuries, to an American hegemony the reply is that the transfer took place in the Second World War, and no amount of effort within Britain's capacity thereafter could have re-established her position. They may console themselves, however, with the thought that part of Britain's role is being taken over by another Commonwealth country—Australia. The interest and commitments of Australia in this area, which for her is the "near north", has been growing steadily. A.N.Z.A.M., A.N.Z.U.S. and S.E.A.T.O. mark the progression. In addition Australia has taken over from Britain the outlying islands in this area which might have some strategic significance. The Cocos-Keeling Islands[1] in the Indian Ocean which were previously administered from Singapore were handed over to Australia in 1955. Christmas Island which lies some 500 miles east of the Cocos, to the south of Java Head, and was also part of the colony of Singapore, became Australian territory in 1958.

In undertaking a more prominent role Australia has an advantage over Britain in that she can claim to belong to the area. Britain's involvement has been open to challenge as imperialist intervention, since it arose out of the possession of dependent territories. But the most ardent anti-colonialist could hardly contest Australia's right to participate in developments in the region.

This shift also fits the requirements of local defence: it is desirable that the means to deal with small-scale aggression should be provided by the countries of the area. In the background, as a safe-

[1] These islands were the setting of a family saga comparable on a smaller scale to that of the Brooke dynasty in Sarawak. John Clunies-Ross settled there in the 1820's, and the family remained in possession until the islands were annexed to the Straits Settlements in 1903. Members of the family were also active in developing phosphate deposits on Christmas Island by means of a company which was bought out by the Australian and New Zealand Governments in 1949.

guard against a major onslaught, lies the ultimate deterrent. Eden has testified to its efficacy at the Geneva Conference. He records:

"This was the first international meeting at which I was sharply conscious of the deterrent power of the hydrogen bomb. I was grateful for it. I do not believe that we should have got through the Geneva Conference and avoided a major war without it."

Granted that safeguard, the most likely contingency to be faced is a local clash, as in Laos, which would best be dealt with by the countries in the area if they were capable of it. This conception was clearly in mind when S.E.A.T.O. was formed: hence the emphasis on strengthening the member countries internally. The limited nature of the steps taken in that direction has been indicated. But a greater limitation is the small Asian membership of S.E.A.T.O.

When the proposal for a defence organization came from the U.S.A., Britain was careful to insist that every effort should be made to bring in as many Asian countries as possible, or at least not to engender their hostility. Eden relates:

"I repeatedly emphasized that although India and other Asian countries might well choose to remain outside such an arrangement, they should nevertheless be given every opportunity to participate and should be kept fully informed. If they could not be with us, we must not put them against us."

The American view, on the other hand, was opposed to the inclusion of India, as that would raise the question of including Formosa as well. In the event the treaty area was limited to the territories of the parties and the general area south of 20° 30", which excluded Formosa and Hong Kong. India was kept out both by the participation of Pakistan and by Nehru's concept of non-alignment, and several of the countries of south-east Asia followed her example. The upshot was that the organization had only three Asian members—Pakistan, Thailand and Philippines. Malaya was included for a time by virtue of Britain's membership; but independent Malaya opted out. Moreover, of the Asian members two —Pakistan and Philippines—are on the fringes of the area, if indeed Pakistan belongs to the area at all. The conclusion must be that, although S.E.A.T.O. has probably limited Communist expansion, it is not firmly based in the region which it is designed to protect.

Is it worth maintaining an organization which lends a handle for accusations of Western imperialism and evokes the antipathy of the "uncommitted" countries? Would it not have been better to develop the five-power Staff Agency? In retrospect this is arguable; but it does not follow that S.E.A.T.O. should be disbanded. Such a step would inevitably be interpreted as a weakening of the resistance to Communism in south-east Asia. Looking forward, which lines of policy show most promise? Surely those which strengthen the Asian component of S.E.A.T.O. or, more generally, strengthen the power of Asian countries to resist Communism.

The likelihood of S.E.A.T.O. acquiring a larger Asian membership is remote. The doctrine of non-alignment preached from Delhi is more persuasive and more attuned to the prevailing temper of anti-colonialism, which was reflected in the grouping of the "Colombo Powers". Like the Colombo Plan it took its name from an inaugural meeting held at Colombo, but was much more limited in membership. The five Asian countries whose Prime Ministers met together in April–May, 1954, at the invitation of the then Prime Minister of Ceylon, Sir John Kotelawala, were India, Pakistan, Ceylon, Burma and Indonesia. Geography provided one link of the association: their location around the Bay of Bengal recalled the earlier connexions of India and the Indies. Malaya was omitted as it was not then independent. Another link was common opposition to colonialism. These common interests brought them together, although between some of them, notably India and Pakistan, there were particular problems which held them apart.

They met in response to the danger which threatened south and south-east Asia from the war in Indo-China, and much of their attention was focused on the Geneva Conference which was in session at the same time. The British Government, for their part, were very conscious of the existence of this group. The Foreign Secretary, Mr. Eden, reporting to the House of Commons on the progress of the Geneva Conference on June 23, 1954, declared:

"Although our Asian partners in the Commonwealth were not represented at the [Geneva] Conference, we were able to keep in constant contact with them at every stage of our work. This also was quite invaluable to us because, in my view, there will never be any real security in South-East Asia without the good-will of the free Asian countries. If peace is ever restored in

Indo-China, then I believe that these countries will be willing to take their part in supervising and guaranteeing the settlement. If so, there will be a good chance for that settlement to last. If also we succeed in negotiating some form of permanent South-East Asia defence organization, it will not be fully effective without the understanding and support of the Colombo Powers."

He also proposed, with French and American support, that the Colombo Powers should act as the Supervisory Commission for the Geneva settlement, but this was declined by the other side. The Colombo Powers did, however, express their satisfaction at the ending of the war in Indo-China, and their "firm support of the Geneva Agreements".

At the next stage, when the creation of S.E.A.T.O. was being considered, the British Government was careful to ask the Colombo Powers for their views. Sir John Kotelawala proposed another meeting, but the Indian Government, committed to its policy of non-alignment, was hostile to the idea of a military pact, and Indonesia and Burma took a similar stand. No other attitude could have have been expected from the Indonesian Government which was dependent on Communist support, but the Burmese reaction was more complex. Although Burma could not contemplate joining S.E.A.T.O. and officially condemned its establishment, unofficially there was some satisfaction in its existence as it brought a feeling of greater security. The Government of Ceylon went further and was "prepared to maintain an open mind on the subject" but declined to join. Only Pakistan became a member of the new organization, but this meant a split in the grouping of the Colombo Powers only a few months after it had been formed.

At the same time, on the initiative of the Prime Minister of Indonesia, Ali Sastroamidjojo, the idea was launched of a wider meeting of African and Asian countries. This proposal was pursued at a further meeting of the Colombo Powers held at Bogor in Indonesia in December, 1954. There the five sponsoring powers drew up a list of invitations. Twenty-five countries were invited from the African and Asian continents. Participation was restricted to countries which were independent, but it did not include them all. Communist China was invited, but not Nationalist China. Both North and South Vietnam were included, but neither North nor South Korea. The Arab states were on the list, but not Israel. The

African states were asked, including the Central African Federation, but not the Union of South Africa. South-east Asia was fully represented, but Australia and New Zealand were left out. The logic of these choices was hard to follow. It resulted from the requirement that invitations should have the unanimous approval of the five sponsoring countries, and so reflected the common denominator of the Colombo Powers.

In the event twenty-four of the countries accepted, and so twenty-nine countries in all forgathered at Bandung in Indonesia in April, 1955. The only refusal came from the Central African Federation. Consequently the conference was entirely "coloured" without any "white" representation. Nevertheless, it proved difficult to reach unanimity. Even on anti-colonialism there was sharp disagreement between those who wanted to condemn only the old imperialism and those who wanted to include the newer form of Communist domination, and an ambiguous form of words had to be found. This disagreement was reflected amongst the south-east Asian participants also; for some of them, notably Cambodia, Thailand and the Philippines, Chinese expansionism was more immediately disturbing than the plight of the Soviet satellites. Nor was there any real agreement on non-alignment. The policy was pressed, but the committed countries would not be moved from their engagements. Again the final communique had to adopt an ambiguous form of words, recognizing the right of each nation to defend itself singly or collectively and at the same time recommending abstention from "arrangements of collective defence to serve the particular interests of any of the big powers".

The British reaction to the Bandung Conference was mixed. If it afforded an opportunity for the representative of Communist China, Mr. Chou En-lai, to show himself conciliatory and co-operative, it enabled other countries to impress upon him the suspicions and fears that were entertained in Asia in regard to Communist China. To the extent that it brought Communist China into greater participation in international relations it was welcomed; to the extent that it gave Communist China a one-sided opportunity of presenting its case it was deplored. Similarly, the gathering of the Afro-Asian States was in itself regarded as unexceptionable provided it was not intended as an anti-Western front. This did not in fact materialize. The anti-Westerners were confronted with the realities of international politics which they were obliged to recognize. It transpired that Afro-Asianism was not sufficient basis for a durable and effective association. Although there has been block voting in the United Nations, it has been neither regular nor uniform and there has been no repeat performance of the Bandung Conference.

There was, however, another meeting of the Colombo Powers held at Delhi in November of 1956 in response to the Suez crisis. On this occasion there was an absentee. The split in the grouping had widened, and the Prime Minister of Pakistan declined to attend. Again the initiative came from Indonesia; but it was largely on the insistence of Burma that the attention of the meeting was not confined to the Suez crisis but extended to include Soviet intervention in Hungary. Thereafter the Colombo Powers grouping, which had by Pakistan's abstention already shed one member, became quiescent if not moribund. Both attempts at regional grouping —whether of Asian or of Afro-Asian countries—petered out, nor did they alter the attitude of south-east Asian countries towards S.E.A.T.O.

An opportunity for S.E.A.T.O. to expand its Asian membership was presented when the Federation of Malaya atttained independence; but the new state did not join. If Malaya shies away no other country is likely to come in, unless there is a radical change in the situation. Yet until the danger of Communist aggression is dispelled, which is a long way off, there is need for a collective guarantee to which Britain is bound to contribute—for one very good reason that the guarantee covers several British territories. Her interests extend beyond those territories to the region as a whole both as a matter of principle and because of its global strategic importance; but they are not matched by her capacity to sustain the effort of military and economic support. If there has to be a choice where should the emphasis be placed?

The balance of the arguments is surely in favour of Britain concentrating on providing economic and technical aid. On the one hand, the amount of military support that Britain can supply at such long range could never be very great, and the facilities available to her in the area are liable to diminish rather than increase. On the other hand, her provision of economic and technical aid although limited in scale has been effective in method. The Colombo Plan is the outstanding example. In contrast to S.E.A.T.O. it has been able to achieve comprehensive membership, including all the countries of south-east Asia and some others besides. There is also the office of Commissioner-General for South-East Asia. The forerunner was Lord Killearn who was sent to Singapore as Special Commissioner in 1946. His task was to fill the administrative gap, in regard to supplies and rehabilitation, left by the winding up of South-East Asia Command. One of his most important contributions was the arrangement of Liaison Conferences for the allocation of rice supplies to avert famine. He was succeeded in 1948 by Malcolm MacDonald who was given the title of Commissioner-General for South-East Asia, while he continued as Governor-General of Malaya. The next appointment, in 1955, was Sir Robert Scott, who was followed in 1960 by Lord Selkirk. Ever since the war, therefore, Britain has had a representative and an office in south-east Asia whose job it was to keep a general lookout over the area and try to achieve a coherent and co-ordinated policy. At the same time the Commissioner-General's office was able to supplement the usual channels for conveying Britain's views to the Governments and peoples of the region. Malcolm Macdonald in particular, during his long term of office, was able to portray the changed attitude of post-war Britain and the desire to replace the old relationship of master and servant by one of equality.

It is precisely because of Britain's willingness to accept this change with good grace and to hasten the ending of empire that her prestige has remained relatively high in the East, making possible the exercise of an important diplomatic role. Having embarked upon this policy there is no turning back, partly because it would be impracticable and partly because it would destroy all the compensatory gain that Britain has acquired from it. The path of British policy marked out in India, Burma and Malaya must be pursued to Singapore and to Borneo. No considerations of the value of the Singapore base should be allowed to block it. Any attempt to seek a Cyprus arrangement would be disastrous. It would not save the base, and would merely lose goodwill. The right policy is the one which is desired by Singapore—union with the Federation. Beyond that there is the incorporation of the Borneo territories in the project, to which the Prime Minister of Malaya has reverted, of "Greater Malaysia". The achievement of such a union as a viable entity with British assistance and support would be a fitting consummation of Britain's expansion to the East.

MALAYSIA

The Malayan Prime Minister's proposal has not met with general enthusiasm. Reactions from British officials in the North Borneo territories were reported to be cool. In Singapore the Left-wing of the ruling party condemned their leader's declared intention of effecting a merger between Singapore and the Federation by 1963 as a "sell-out", and demanded instead full self-government for Singapore. This policy was espoused also by David Marshall, the former Chief Minister, who now heads the Workers' Party. At a by-election in July, 1961, he succeeded in defeating a Malay candidate nominated by the P.A.P. The weight of the Trade Union Congress, controlled by Left-wing dissidents, was thrown into the scales against the Government.

There was some speculation at first that the Tunku was trying to call in the North Borneo territories to redress the balance which would be upset in favour of the Chinese by the merger with Singapore. But urgency was added by the challenge from the extreme Left in Singapore, organized in the Socialist Front, while the official response from the North Borneo territories remained tepid. It was a measure of the growing self-confidence of Malaya that the Tunku decided to press on with the Singapore merger as the first stage. The two Prime Ministers met for discussions in September, 1961, and agreed on a target date for the merger in June, 1963. The Prime Minister of Singapore, Lee Kuan Yew, accused Britain of putting difficulties in the way of the merger out of concern for the S.E.A.T.O. bases on the island. The Tunku prepared to go to London for talks with the British Government, and before his departure received a message from the British Prime Minister, Mr. Macmillan, that

"There is a wide measure of agreement between us on this plan of Malaysia, in that the British Government would welcome and accept the concept of a Malaysia which would incorporate the Federation of Malaya, Singapore, and the three Borneo territories."

But the question of the bases remained unsettled.

The London talks, to general surprise, appeared to end in full agreement not merely about Malaysia but also about the bases. A commission was appointed to ascertain the views of the people of

North Borneo and Sarawak, and a joint statement declared that the future Government of the Federation of Malaysia would afford to the British Government the right to continue to maintain bases at Singapore

"for the purpose of assisting in the defence of Malaysia, and for Commonwealth defence and for the preservation of peace in South-East Asia."

This was interpreted in London as meaning that Britain would be able to continue using the bases for S.E.A.T.O. purposes; but back in Malaya the Tunku assured the Prime Minister of Singapore that Malaysia would have a veto :

"The agreement reached between us and Britain on the use of the Singapore base is only an extension of the existing agreement with Britain. It permits the use of the base, as provided under the terms of the treaty, only with the agreement of the future Malaysia Government—but not as a right. The British Government and ourselves emphasized that the Singapore base is not a S.E.A.T.O. base."

Here was an apparent conflict of interpretation, but the Tunku was unperturbed. With disarming frankness he explained—

"The communique gives us the chance to explain it away to our different parliaments"

and he expatiated on the virtues of ambiguity.[1] But about the formation of Malaysia he was more precise. In particular the merger with Singapore was urgent because, if there were a change of Government there, the project would be halted. But the merger could not be effected unless the North Borneo territories (North Borneo and Sarawak) were included from the first. If the target date remained at June, 1963, this meant a very rapid political development in Borneo. It remained to be seen whether there was agreement between the British and Malayan Governments on this point or whether, like the Singapore bases, it was shrouded in ambiguity.

[1] Later, in January, 1962, he added another gloss: "Singapore is a British base and therefore Britain can use it as she likes. However, for courtesy reasons, she would consult the Government of Malaysia before doing this."

15

RETROSPECT AND PROSPECT

IN the centuries which have elapsed since the first merchant venturers set sail in quest of the riches of the East, Britain's relations with south-east Asia have gone through several phases of expansion and contraction. In the first phase which was inaugurated under the auspices of the first Queen Elizabeth, the main object was trade, and the factories which were planted in the Indies were designed not as imperial outposts but simply as trading posts. Even so the intervention of English traders met with opposition from the Dutch, and they were obliged to yield to the superior strength and determination of their competitors. After the "massacre of Amboina" the English turned their attention from the Indies to India, with only desultory interest in the lands which lay between. During this period Britain's involvement in south-east Asia was chiefly with Burma and Siam and had a different motivation. Strategic considerations took priority over trade.

Strategy was the dominant factor in launching the second wave of British expansion which began with the acquisition of Penang in 1786. But it was never the sole motive. Strategy, after all, is only a means to an end, never an end in itself. Its constant object from Britain's viewpoint is the protection of her interests. At the end of the eighteenth century her main interests in the East were the Indian empire and the China trade. These, together with the strategic requirements for their protection, were the mainsprings of British imperialism in south-east Asia during the nineteenth century. The acquisition of Burma was partly to defend the north-east frontier of India and partly to open an overland trade route to China. The security of the Eastern trade was the argument which enabled Raffles to establish his foothold on Singapore, to become the base from which Britain's sway was extended in the Malay peninsula and Borneo. One acquisition led to another. It has been observed that a large empire is the best reason for a larger empire. To protect one territory it was thought necessary to prevent adjacent lands from falling under the control of another power. So the process continued fom territory to territory, from protectorate to annexation. Alternatively, disorder and lawlessness in areas impinging upon territories for which Britain had become responsible called for intervention, and it proved less difficult to enter than to withdraw. A constant factor in this process was the altruistic belief of the Victorian era that Britain had an obligation to bring the benefits of civilization to the primitive heathen.

By the end of the century Britain's dominion had almost reached its maximum extent in south-east Asia. Burma was conquered; the Straits Settlements were colonized; the Malay states were federated; the Borneo territories were protected. Only the four northern Malay states remained to be detached from Siam in 1909. Thereafter for two generations Britain held sway over much of the region. During that time an imposing edifice of administrative, economic and military power was constructed. Its collapse was catastrophic. The whole structure was demolished by the lightning campaign of the Japanese.

The Greater East Asia Co-prosperity Sphere failed to establish a new order, but it effectively put an end to the old. The third phase of British expansion was designed to restore the position which had been thus overturned. By the final victory in the Second World War Britain was able to return to the territories from which she had been ejected. But things could never be the same again. Just as the Japanese victory in the war against Russia in 1905 heralded the rise of the nationalist movement in the East, so the Japanese victory in 1942 meant the end of Western empire in southern Asia. The old régime was restored for a time but could not be maintained.

The post-war years saw the application of two contrary policies in south-east Asia, represented on the one hand by the Dutch and French, who endeavoured to retain their Asian possessions with the minimum of concessions, and on the other by the British who sought, by the timely grant of self-government, to substitute partnership for imperialism. It has often been argued that Britain could do no other. This may be true; but it was true also for France and the Netherlands, yet it did not stop them from trying to hang on. Britain too might have adopted a policy which would have meant greater expenditure of money and men with less result, had it not been for the combination of Mountbatten as Supreme Commander in south-east Asia and a timely switch of policy by the Government at Westminster.

The transfer of power has been accomplished in the case of

Burma and of Malaya, but Britain still retains responsibility for and control of territories in the area and has obligations to neighbouring countries. This position presents a choice of policies. One course of action is ruled out. It is no longer possible to contemplate the full restoration of the *status quo ante bellum*. That was the ambition of some after the Second World War, but what has happened since has put it out of reach. The alternatives available to Britain in the second post-war decade are much more limited.

There are broadly three possibilities. The first is to attempt to hang on to those possessions which remain, and to preserve what is left of Britain's former position. For this there are two requirements. One is a policy of "divide and rule" applied to Malaya, Singapore and Borneo—which would be feasible for a time. Indeed, it is difficult to avoid in an area with such a racial mixture, since any policy is liable to favour one group as against another. The other requirement would be a much greater effort—political, economic, cultural and military—than Britain is now putting into this region. This too is feasible, but it would necessarily be at the expense of other British commitments. Such a policy is conceivable; but its morality is questionable and it would clearly be misguided. It would destroy the credit which Britain has gained from her policy of divesting herself of empire in the East since the war, and could not be successful in the long run although it might succeed in maintaining Britain's position for a number of years. The question is whether that extension, which could not be very long, is worth the animosity and the cost that it would involve. The answer must surely be that it is not.

At the other extreme is the policy of cutting Britain's losses and pulling out. If her position cannot in the long run be maintained, why spend men and money on it? Would it not be better to cast off her responsibilities in south-east Asia, recognizing that it is for others to shoulder a burden which has now surpassed her capacity, and concentrate her limited resources on vital needs nearer home? This is a policy of despair. Granted that in the long run the trend is towards her departure from the East, that is not to say that in the nearer future Britain has no contribution to make and has no responsibilities to fulfil. The argument for quitting was one that was used when the emergency began in Malaya. It is undoubtedly true that British lives and money would have been saved by evacuating and leaving Malaya to her fate; but Malaya would now be under

Communist rule. The success in meeting the emergency provides the proof that Britain can still contribute something. British rule in Malaya has been succeeded not by Communist domination but by a democracy which appears as one of the healthiest in the East. Britain has a similar duty towards her remaining possessions and there is no reason to suppose that she is any more incapable of performing it. In addition, her role at the Geneva Conference and in the general diplomacy of the area has by no means been negligible. Events since the war provide no justification for a policy of abandonment.

If these two courses are rejected, the third choice is the policy which has been followed hitherto. It is a programme of progressive withdrawal, leaving behind the basis upon which viable independent and democratic states can be built. It means acceptance of the continuing but gradual decline of Britain's position in south-east Asia, although it could be compensated by the growth of cultural and economic relations which it is within her capacity to foster. Her contribution to the military security of the area must necessarily be small, but her part in economic and technical aid, particularly educational development, could be enormously important.

The prospect of Britain joining the European Economic Community reinforces the argument for this line of policy. That step cannot in the long run fail to loosen the ties of the Commonwealth still further. They have been relaxing since the war, in south-east Asia as elsewhere. As Britain moves into Europe, which appears to be the direction that she is taking willy-nilly, there is still greater need to concentrate on the policy of guiding the remaining dependencies in south-east Asia towards full self-government. One of the main objections in Asian eyes to Britain's joining Europe is that she will thereby be linked with countries still branded with the stigma of imperialism. It is all the more necessary for Britain to demonstrate by her actions that her own outlook and policy remains unchanged.

The most promising line of advance is one which bases itself on Malaya as the main pillar of a regional grouping in south-east Asia. The desirable outcome would be a grouping of Malaya, Singapore and the Borneo territories in some form of closer association. This is the policy favoured by the Malayan Government. The main objection is liable to come, as has been shown, from Brunei; but there will be difficulties in the other territories also. It is here that Britain still has an important role to play. Perhaps the most valuable parting gift that Britain could make to south-east Asia would be in preparing the way for the territories of Borneo and Singapore to join up with Malaya.

Beyond that, it is in the interest of Britain as of the non-Communist world generally, to strengthen and associate more closely all the independent countries of south-east Asia. But in that wider field Britain's influence is necessarily more limited. In regard to the Commonwealth countries of the area a choice of policies is still open to Britain. It should be governed by the principle which Lord Minto recommended to Raffles 150 years ago—"While we are here, let us do all the good we can".

SELECT BIBLIOGRAPHY

G. C. ALLEN and A. G. DONNITHORNE, *Western Enterprise in Indonesia and Malaya* (London, 1957).

J. CADY, *History of Modern Burma* (New York, 1958).

H. G. CALLIS, *Foreign Capital in South-East Asia* (New York, 1942).

F. S. CHAPMAN, *The Jungle is Neutral* (London, 1949).

J. L. CHRISTIAN, *Modern Burma* (California, 1942).

W. S. CHURCHILL, *Second World War* (London, 1948–54).

M. COLLIS, *Last and First in Burma* (London, 1956).

C. D. COWAN, *Nineteenth-Century Malaya* (London, 1961).

F. S. V. DONNISON, *Public Administration in Burma* (London, 1932); *British Military Administration in the Far East* (London, 1943).

W. G. EAST and O. H. K. SPATE (*eds.*), *Changing Map of Asia* (London, 1950).

A. EDEN, *Full Circle* (London, 1960).

J. EHRMAN, *Grand Strategy,* Vols. V & VI (London, 1956).

R. EMERSON, *Representative Government in South-East Asia* (Harvard, 1955).

FEDERATION OF BRITISH INDUSTRIES, *A Trade in Transition* (London, 1961).

R. H. FIFIELD, D*iplomacy of South-East Asia 1945–58* (New York, 1958).

W. FOSTER, *England's Quest of Eastern Trade* (London, 1933).

J. S. FURNIVALL, *Colonial Policy and Practice* (Cambridge, 1948).

R. GRENFELL, *Main Fleet to Singapore* (London, 1951).

E. M. GULL, *British Economic Interests in the Far East* (London, 1943).

D. G. E. HALL, *History of South-East Asia* (London, 1955); *Burma* (London, 1950).

R. HAKLUYT, *Principal Navigations of the English Nation.*

B. HARRISON, *South-East Asia* (London, 1955).

G. E. HARVEY, *British Rule in Burma* (London, 1946).

F. C. JONES, *Japan's New Order in East Asia* (London, 1954).

S. W. JONES, *Public Administration in Malaya* (London, 1953).

G. McT. KAHIN, *The Asian-African Conference, Bandung* (New York, 1956).

BIBLIOGRAPHY

J. D. LANCASTER, *Emancipation of French Indo-China* (London, 1961).

MAUNG MAUNG, *Burma in the Family of Nations* (Amsterdam, 1957).

L. A. MILLS, *British Rule in Eastern Asia* (London, 1942); *Malaya* (London, 1958).

LORD MOUNTBATTEN, *Report by S.A.C.S.E.A.* (London, 1951).

A. S. B. OLVER, *British Policy in East and South-eastern Asia 1945–50* (London, 1950).

A. E. PERCIVAL, *The War in Malaya* (London, 1949).

V. PURCELL, *Malaya: Communist or Free?* (London, 1954).

LADY RAFFLES, *Memoir of Sir T. S. Raffles* (London, 1830).

W. D. REEVE, *Public Administration in Siam* (London, 1952).

ROYAL INSTITUTE OF INTERNATIONAL AFFAIRS, *Collective Defence in South-East Asia* (London, 1956).

S. RUNCIMAN, *White Rajahs* (Cambridge, 1960).

T. H. SILCOCK, *Commonwealth Economy in South-East Asia* (London, 1959).

F. A. SWETTENHAM, *British Malaya* (London, 1948).

H. TINKER, *Union of Burma* (London, 1957).

K. G. TREGONNING, *Under Chartered Company Rule* (Singapore, 1958).

W. F. VELLA, *Impact of the West on Government in Thailand* (Berkeley, 1955).

J. A. WILLIAMSON, *The Ocean in English History* (Oxford, 1941).

R. WINSTEDT, *Malaya and its History* (London, 1948).

C. E. WURTZBURG, *Raffles of the Eastern Isles* (London, 1954).

INDEX

Abdul Rahman, Tunku, 73, 82, 132, 138, 146, 184, 193–4
Abdul Razak, Dato, 142
Achin, 18–19, 27, 35
Aid, economic and technical, 171–5
Alor Star, 73, 132
Amarapura, 41
Amboina, 20, 195
America (U.S.A.), 55–56, 72, 84, 87, 89–90, 95–96, 100, 103–6, 110, 123, 136, 151, 159, 163, 166, 173, 175, 178–9, 184, 187
American Seventh Fleet, 185–6
American Trading Company of Borneo, 56
Amery, Leopold, 83
Angkor, 10
Anglo-Burmese war:
first, 41–42
second, 46–47
third, 62, 68
Anglo-Dutch Treaty, (1824), 44
Anglo-Dutch war, 20, 23
Anglo-German Naval Agreement, (1935), 84
Anglo-Japanese Alliance, 84
Anglo-Oriental (Malaya) Corporation, 63, 135
Anglo-Siamese Treaty (1909), 53
Annam, 10
Anti-Fascist People's Freedom League (A.F.P.F.L.), 100, 109, 112–21
A.N.Z.A.M., 184, 186
A.N.Z.U.S., 166, 186
Arakan, 39, 41, 47
Assam, 41, 44
Association of South-East Asian States (A.S.A.S.) – (A.S.A.), 138
Attlee, 116–17

Attlee-Aung San Agreement, 117–18
Attlee-Nu Agreement, 122, 124
Aung San, 69, 98, 100–1, 110, 112–19
Australia, 84–86, 95, 105, 149, 151–3, 163, 166, 184, 186, 190
Ava, 24, 39, 41
Ayub Khan, 182
Ayuthia, 10, 19–20, 23
Azahari, 152

Ba Maw, 100, 102
Bali, 33
Balambangan, 27
Banda, 20
Banka, 36
Bandung, 190
Conference, 190–1
Bangkok, 23, 42, 55, 65, 74, 158, 181, 184
Banjarmassin, 20
Bantam, 19–20, 22–23
Bao Dai, 165
Baptists, 68
Batambang, 55
Batavia, 160–2
Bencoolen, 22, 34, 37
Bengal, 41
Bengal, Bay of, 19, 23, 27, 104–5, 188
Bevin, Mr., 161
Bhamo, 47–48
Bintang, 34
Bogor, 189
Bombay Burmah Trading Corporation, 48, 55, 62
Borneo, 20, 33, 43–44, 55–57, 82, 106, 146–57, 164, 184–5, 192, 195–9
North, 57, 61, 80, 102, 138–9, 150–2, 174–5, 193–4

Borneo, North—*contd.*
— civil service, 152
— education in, 72–73
— government, 80, 152
— investment in, 151
— population, 151
— trade with, 151, 176–7
North, Trading Company, 151
Borobodur, 10
Bottomley, Arthur, 118
Briggs Plan, 131
British Broadcasting Corporation, 172
British Burmah Petroleum Company, 62
British Council, 171–2
British North Borneo Company, 56–57, 147, 150–1
Brooke:
James, 43–44, 56–57
dynasty, 80, 147–8
Brunei, 44, 56–57, 61, 80, 138, 145, 147, 150, 152–6, 160, 198
government, 153–4
population, 153
trade, 153
Sultan of, 44, 153–4
Brunei Shell Petroleum Co. Ltd., 153
Buddhism, 10
Burma, 10, 16, 22, 24–25, 37–41, 42, 43, 44–49, 55, 74, 87, 98–104, 109–26, 129, 135–6, 157–8, 165, 174, 178, 188–9, 191–2, 195–7
civil service, 81
conquest of, 44–49
education in, 67–70, 123
government, 76–77, 124
investment in, 61–63, 121–2, 175
Japanese occupation, 100–1
trade with 64, 122, 176
Burma Chamber of Commerce, 76
Burma Corporation, 62
Burma Estates, 62

Burma, Government of, Act, 77
Burma Independence Army, 118
Burma National Army, 101
Burma Road, 87–88, 91
Burmah Oil Company, 62, 121
Burney, Captain, 42–43
Burney Treaty, 55
Butterworth, 185

Cachar, 41
Calcutta, 28, 30, 34–35, 41–42
Calcutta University, 68
Calicut, 11
Cambodia, 33, 157–8, 166, 172, 174, 190
Canning, 35
Cape of Good Hope, 16, 34
Castlereagh, 35, 37
Celebes, 106
Central Office of Information, 172
Ceylon, 122, 165, 173, 188–9
Chamberlain, J., 57
Chamberlain, N., 85
Champa, 10
Chiefs of Staff, 88, 104–5, 110–11, 126–8, 164
Chiengmai, 16
China, 15–16, 27, 34, 36–37, 39, 47–49, 72, 87, 89, 101, 104, 127, 159, 166, 176, 179, 189–90, 195
Ching Peng, 128
Chittagong, 41
Chou En-lai, 190
Christmas Island, 139, 186
Chungking, 87
Chulalongkorn, 73
Chulalongkorn University, 74
Churchill:
Lord Randolph, 48
Winston, 86, 88, 95, 104–5, 117, 186
Clarke, Sir Andrew, 50
Cobbold, Lord, 156
Cobden, 46–47
Cochin China, 33
Cocos Islands, 139, 186

Colombo Plan, 122–3, 125, 134, 151–2, 163, 173–5, 178, 181–2, 188, 191
Colombo Powers, 188–91
Colonial Development Corporation, 135
Colonial Development & Welfare Fund, 149, 151, 174
Committee of Imperial Defence, 84–85
Commonwealth, 117, 133, 136–7, 166, 173, 175, 177–8, 198
Communism, 98, 126–9, 133, 143, 149, 163, 165–6, 173, 179, 181–2, 188, 198
Consolidated Tin Smelters, 66
Cooper, Duff, 74
Coromandel coast, 23–24
Corregidor, 96
Cox, Captain, 39

Dalhousie, Lord, 46
D'Argenlieu, Admiral Thierry, 164
Dayaks, 102, 150
Decoux, Admiral, 103
Dent Brothers, 56
Department of Technical Co-operation, 174
Diana, 43
Dilke, 57
Dill, Sir John, 88, 91
Disraeli, 56
Djakarta, 20, 172
Dobbie, General, 85
Dorman-Smith, Sir Reginald, 113–16
Drake, Sir Francis, 15–16
Dusuns, 152
Dutch, 11, 19–20, 22–23, 27, 29–30, 32–37, 102, 106, 160–3, 179, 195–6
Dutch East Indies, 89–90, 95–96, 102, 160
  investment in, 63
  trade with, 65

East India Company, 15, 18–20, 22–25, 27–29, 31–36, 39, 42, 44, 56, 61

East Indies, 15–16, 19, 22, 27, 37, 102, 105, 159, 179, 188, 195
Eden, Sir Anthony, 166, 187–8
Education in:
  Borneo, 72–73
  Burma, 67–70
  Malaya, 70–72
Elizabeth I, 15, 18, 195
English language, 67, 123–4, 137, 140–1, 143–4, 150, 152–3, 167, 171–3, 178
European Common Market, 136, 198

Factories, 19–22
Fitch, Ralph, 16
Formosa, 187
France, 23–24, 27–28, 32, 39, 43, 48, 55, 106, 164–6, 184, 196
Frontier Areas Committee, 118
Funan, 10

Geneva Conference, 166, 187–8, 198
Gladstone, 48, 56–57
Globe, 19
Goa, 11
Government in Borneo, 80, 152
  Burma, 76–77, 124
  Malaya, 77–80, 129–30
Gracey, Major-General, 164
Granville, 57
Greater East Asia Ministry, 99
Gurney, Sir Henry, 131

Hague Conference, 163
Hainan, 106
Hakluyt, 16
Hamilton, Captain Alexander, 36
Hastings, Lrd, 34
Hinduism, 9
Hong Kong, 44, 72, 106, 145, 149, 159, 166, 185, 187

India, 19, 22–23, 25, 27, 33, 39, 42, 48, 51, 68, 72, 76, 85, 87, 105, 115, 117, 122, 144, 165, 179, 187–9, 192, 195
  Act (1784), 27

India—*contd.*
  Board of Control, 32, 35
  Governor-General of, 32–36, 39, 46
  Government of, 41–43, 46–49, 76
  Government of, Act, 77
  Presidency of, 49
  Viceroy of, 48
Indian National Army, 101
India Ocean, 86, 105, 186
Indo-Burma Petroleum Co., 62
Indo-China, 22, 55, 62, 90, 95, 103, 106, 164–7, 172, 179, 188–9
  trade with, 166, 177
Indomitable, 96
Indonesia, 50, 61, 99, 101–2, 138, 144, 151, 159–64, 172, 174, 188–91
  investment in, 163, 175
  trade with, 163, 176–7
Irrawaddy, 10, 48
Irrawaddy Flotilla Company, 121
Islam, 11
Ismay, General, 89, 91

Jambi, 20
James II, 23–24
Japan, 16, 84–85, 88–89, 95–96, 99–100, 104–6, 122, 128, 144, 151–2, 176
Japan's New Order, 95–104
Java, 9–10, 20, 22, 29, 31–34, 96, 106, 152, 160–62
Jesselton, 102, 150, 160
Johore, 35–36, 53
Joint Planning Staff, 106
Junkseylon, 27

Karens, 68, 118
Karimata Straits, 32
Kedah, 27–28, 42–43, 53, 73, 132
Kedazans, Society of, 152
Kelantan, 43, 53
Kerr, Sir Archibald Clarke, 161
Khmers, 10
Khuang Aphaiwongse, 103

Killearn, Lord, 158, 162, 192
Kimberley, Lord, 50
Kotelawala, Sir John, 188–9
Korea, 189
Kra Isthmus, 10, 158
Kuala Lumpur, 53, 137, 144
Kuching, 160
Kuomintang, 126–7

Labuan, 44, 56–57, 80, 139, 147, 152, 160
Lambert, Commodore, 46
Lancaster, James, 18–19
Langkasuka, 10
Laos, 146, 157–8, 166, 172, 174, 183–5, 187
Ledo, 104
Lee Kuan Yew, 142, 193
Leonowens, Mrs., 73
Lim Yew Hock, 141
Linggadjati Agreement, 162
Lingga, 33
Light, Francis, 27–28
Ligor, Raja, of, 42
London Chamber of Commerce, 48
London Tin Corporation, 63
Low, Captain, 43
Lutong, 149–50

MacArthur, General, 106
MacDonald, Maclcolm, 165, 192
MacMichael, Sir Harold, 129–30, 148
Macmillan, Harold, 193
Macassar, 20, 22
Madras, 23–24, 27–28
Majapahit, 10, 32
Malacca, 10–11, 16, 23, 29–32, 35–37, 43, 49, 86, 139, 184
  Straits of, 34, 37
Malay Administration Service, 81
Malay Peninsula, 16, 19–20, 27, 37, 42–43, 88–90, 105–6, 195
Malay States, 49–52, 55, 103, 157
  Federated, 53, 71, 77, 79, 81, 86, 129, 196
  Unfederated, 77, 79, 81–82, 86, 129, 196

Malaya, 27, 49–53, 61, 63, 66, 85–89, 91, 96, 104, 110, 122, 126–38, 148, 153, 156–9, 164–6, 172, 175–6, 184, 187–8, 192, 197–9
  British Association of, 178
  citizenship, 131, 133
  civil service, 81–82, 131
  economic aid, 134–5
  education in, 70–72, 137
  emergency, 131, 134, 197–8
  government, 77–80, 129–30
  investment in, 62–63, 135, 175
  Japanese occupation, 101
  trade with, 64–65, 136–7
  University of, 134, 137, 144
Malayan:
  Chinese Association, 132
  Civil Service, 81, 130
  Communist Party, 126–9, 130–31
  Democratic Union, 128
  Federation, 140–6, 193
  General Labour Union, 128
  Indian Congress, 132
  People's Anti-Japanese Army (M.P.A.J.A.), 126–8
  People's Anti-Japanese Union (M.P.A.J.U.), 126–7
  Union, 129–30, 139–40
'Malaysia' 156, 192–4
Malaysians, 9
Manila Treaty, 159, 182, 184
Manipur, 41
Mandalay, 47–48, 97
  University of, 172
Marco Polo, 10
Marshall, David, 141, 193
Mediterranean, 85–88, 95
Mekong River, 55
Menam River, 55
Mergui, 23–24
Ming dynasty, 10
Minto, Lord, 30–34, 41, 199
Miri, 149
Moluccas, 15, 30–31, 33
Mongkut, King, 55, 73

Mongol dynasty, 10
Montagu-Chelmsford reforms, 76
Montagu Declaration, 76
Mons, 10, 24
van Mook, 162
Morant, Robert, 73
Morib, 128
Morley-Minto Reforms, 76
Mountbatten, 106, 110–13, 115–17, 126–9, 147, 157, 159–61, 164, 196

Nanyang University, 144
Negrais, 24–25, 39
Negri Sembilam, 52
Newall, Sir Cyril, 88
New Guinea, 57, 157, 163
New Zealand, 84–85, 95, 149, 152, 166, 184, 190
Norrington Committee, 173
Nu, U, 69, 118, 120, 122

Ottoman Turks, 11
Overbeck, 56

Pacific, 15, 89–90, 104–5
Padang, 34, 36
Pagan, 10
Pahang, 52
Pakistan, 144, 181–2, 187–9, 191
Palembang, 34
Palmerston, 44
Pan-Malayan Islamic Party, 138
Pangkor engagement (1874), 51
Panglong Conference, 117
Party Negara, 148
Party Ra'ayat, 152, 154
Patani, 19–20
Pauncefote, Sir Julian, 56
Paya Lebar, 175
Pearl Harbour, 90, 95–96
Pegu, 17, 39, 46–47
Peking Government, 166
Penang, 27–30, 42, 49, 55, 73, 86, 98, 139, 195
  Chamber of Commerce, 79
  Free School, 132

INDEX

People's Action Party (P.A.P.), 142–4, 146, 193
Perak, 43, 51–52
Percival, Lieutenant-General, 86
Perlis, 53
Pethick-Lawrence, Lord, 114–15
Phaulkon, 23–24
Philippines, 11, 50, 96, 99, 106, 138, 151, 156, 181, 187, 190
  investment in, 62
  trade with, 65, 177
Pitt, 27
Pibul Songgram, 103
Pirates, 43–44
Pondicherry, 23–24
Population in:
  Brunei, 153
  Borneo, North, 151
  Burma, 123
  Malaya, 131
  Sarawak, 150
  Singapore, 140–1, 143
Port Dickson, 85
Portuguese, 11, 16, 18–20, 23
Potsdam Conference, 128
Pound, Sir Dudley, 88
Pridi, Regent, 103, 157
Prince of Wales, 96
Province Wellesley, 28, 42

Rama V, 73
Rama VI, 74
Rance, Major-General, 116
Raffles, Sir Thomas, 28–37, 41, 44, 61, 70, 139, 158, 195, 199
Raffles College, 37, 71–72, 142
Rangoon, 39, 41, 46, 74, 87, 96, 104–5, 109, 112, 114, 139, 172
  College, 68
  Students' Union, 69
  Traders' Association, 76
  University of, 69
Rees-Williams, Mr., 118
Reid Commission, 133
Rendel Commission, 140
Repulse, 96

Rhio, 27, 33, 35
Rice Organization, 158
Roosevelt, President, 90, 105
Royal Dutch Shell, 62, 150
Royalist, 44

Sagaing, 97
Saigon, 90, 159, 164–5, 172
Salisbury, Lord, 56
San Filippe, 16, 18
Sandakan, 150, 160
Sandys, Duncan, 145
Sarawak, 44, 56, 61, 80, 102, 138, 147–50, 153–4, 156, 174–5, 194
  education in, 150
  government, 80, 148
  investment in, 149–50
  Overseas Chinese Democratic Youth League, 149
  population, 150
  Shell Oilfields, 149
  trade with, 149, 176
  United People's Party, 148–9
Sastroamidjojo, Ali, 189
Saw, U, 118
Scott, Sir Robert, 145, 192
Selangor, 52
Selkirk, Lord, 192
Semarang, 160
Sematan Bauxite Ltd., 150
Seria Oilfields, 153
Seven Years War, 24, 27
Shanghai, 87
Shan States, 103, 157
Shipping, 18, 65
Shoe Question, 47, 74–75
Shwe Dagon pagoda, 74
Siam, 16, 19–20, 22–23, 33, 41–43, 51, 53–55, 96, 101, 103, 134, 138, 157–9, 172, 174, 181–2, 187, 190, 195–9
  education in 73–74
  investment in 61–62
  trade with, 65, 159, 176–7
Sibuco River, 56
Siemreap, 55

207

INDEX

Simla, 121

Singapore, 32, 34–37, 43–44, 49–50, 61, 65, 104–5, 126, 128–9, 133–4, 138–47, 149, 153, 156, 158, 164, 172, 174–5, 177, 185, 192–3, 196–9

Singapore Base, 83–89, 90–92, 95–96, 145–6, 185–6, 192, 194

  Chamber of Commerce, 50, 79

  citizenship, 141

  education in, 143–4

  government, 140–42

  population, 139, 143–4

  Socialist front, 193

  trade, 144–5, 176

  Workers' Party, 193

Sjahrir, 162

Slim, Lord, 97, 110

South-East Asia Command (S.E.A.C.) 157, 160, 165, 192

South-East Asia Treaty Organization (S.E.A.T.O.), 137–8, 145–6, 159, 166, 175, 181–9, 191, 193–4

South-East Asian Economic and Friendship Treaty, 138

Special Operations Executive, 109, 126

Spice trade, 15–16, 19

Srivijaya, 10

Stephens, Donald, 152

Sterling Area, 136

Straits Settlements, 49–51, 53, 57, 71, 79–81, 129, 133, 139, 196

Straits Settlements Civil Service, 81

Straits Trading Co., 66

Strategy, 83–92, 104–7, 181–94, 195

Subhas Bose, 101

Suez Canal, 49, 91, 191

Sukadana, 20

Sulu, 33, 56, 156

Sumatra, 10, 18–20, 22, 33–34, 106, 157

Sunda, Straits of, 34

Sungei Ujong, 52

Sukarno, 102, 152, 160

Surabaya, 160–61

Symes, Captain, 39, 41

Syriam, 24

Taiping, 85

Tamils, 71

Templer, General, 131

Temenggong of Singapore, 32, 35

Tenasserim, 41–43, 47

Ternate, 15

Thai, 10

Thailand—see Siam

Thakin Nu, 100

Than Tun, 114

Thibaw, King, 47–48

Tiku, 19

Tojo, Premier, 99–100

Tongking, 9

Trade, 64–66, 122, 149, 151, 163, 175–77 (see also individual countries)

Trengganu, 43, 53

Tripartite Pact, 87

United Malays National Organization (U.M.N.O.), 130–2

United Nations, 158, 162, 174

Vajiravudh School, 74

Vasco da Gama, 11

Viet Minh, 103, 164–5, 183

Vietnam, 164, 166, 172, 181, 183

  North, 173, 189

  South, 167, 189

Washington Conference (1921), 83

Wellesley, Duke of Wellington, 28

Western New Guinea, 163

Western Irian, 163–4

Westminster, Treaty of (1654), 20

White, Samuel, 23

Yandabo, Treaty of (1826), 41, 44

Yang di-Pertuan Negara, 141

Young Men's Buddhist Association, 74

Yunnan, 47

DATE DUE

DEC 14 '66			